THE
THUNDER
OF HIS
POWER

THE THUNDER OF HIS POWER

by George Otis

Bible Voice Publishers
Van Nuys, California

Dedication

To Don and Linda Posto for their manifold contributions and unflagging insistence this manuscript be published.

"His word was in my heart as a burning, and I could not forbear telling of it."

—Jeremiah 20:9

Table of Contents

Foreword   9
Introduction   11
1. Roots   13
2. The Sky Is Falling   19
3. The Thunder of God   25
4. The Finney Formula   31
5. Revival or Ashes   37
6. The Dynamic of Commitment   41
7. Portraits of God   47
8. The Beauty of Holiness   55
9. The Secret of Balance   63
10. About Judging   73
11. The Little Foxes   83
12. Human Rights   93
13. The Club of Rome   107

Foreword

Do not read this book if you are content to live with a "do not disturb" sign on the door handle of your life. Do not read it if you are unwilling for challenge and change. Do not go through its pages if mediocrity is acceptable.

However, if you have an ear for music and are willing to hear the blow of the trumpet: Listen! If you are a person who is grateful to God for every watchman He places on the walls to give warning, exhortation and counsel, you will be grateful to Him for this book, *THE THUNDER OF HIS POWER.* Openly and fearlessly George Otis expresses his feelings in the current spiritual climate: the fear of a missing content in renewal; the fear of people being sign-followers, tape addicts, and chronic conventioneers; the fear of lack of depth, lack of a fear of God and the danger of little foxes which spoil the vine. The author's intensity of desire for revival proclaims one of revival's greatest needs—Holiness.

Holiness, which is God's standard of living, "Be ye holy, for I am holy"; "holiness without which no man shall see God"; holiness, which is the very nature and character of God and should be the mark of all who claim to be His children through faith in Christ; holiness which is to hate evil and love righteousness; holiness which is the highway in revival, "A highway shall be there, and a way, and it shall be called the way of holiness. . . ." (Isa. 35:8)

Holiness which struck fear into wicked King Herod's heart because he perceived it in the greatest prophet born of woman, John the Baptist, "For Herod feared John, knowing that he was a just man and a holy ..." (Mark 6:20); holiness which the Shunammite woman saw in the life of Elisha the prophet, causing her to say, "I perceive that this is a holy man of God, which passeth by us continually" (II Kings 4:9); holiness which can exalt this nation—lack of it can destroy it.

THE THUNDER OF HIS POWER contains a very much needed message. I recommend you read it prayerfully, thoughtfully, and obediently, with a renewed understanding of the purpose of your calling as Paul stated in Ephesians 1:4, "According as he hath chosen us in him before the foundation of the world, that we should be holy and without blame before him in love ..."; and a renewed appreciation of the great desire of our wonderful Lord, "to present you holy and unblamable and unreprovable in his sight" (Colossians 1:22).

I know this book will help you to have a holy day, a holy life, and a holy eternity, when we, no doubt, will continually take up the refrain of the song of Moses, "Who is like unto thee, O Lord ... who is like thee, glorious in holiness, fearful in praises, doing wonders?" (Exodus 15:11).

> Revive thy work, O Lord,
> Thy mighty arm make bare
> Speak with the voice that wakes the dead
> And let Thy people hear.

by Campbell McAlpine

Introduction

How wonderful! "BORN AGAIN" emblazoned across the cover of *Newsweek* magazine! Suddenly the good news had become BIG news. Many Christians weren't sure what to make of it. Skepticism suggested it was a case of *deja vu*—a flashback perhaps to the heyday of the Jesus movement in the early '70s.

It didn't take long, however, before the reality of it all began to sink in. Like a dazed starlet in front of popping flashbulbs, the church with all its shy and innocent veneer was learning to revel in the publicity. George Gallup poured fuel on the flames when he announced that more than one-third of adult Americans now claimed a "born again" experience. It had become fashionable to talk about Jesus in public.

Church attendance was on the rise, religious organizations and missions were proliferating at an astonishing rate. Christian literature found its way onto bookracks and newsstands across the country and Christian television finally "arrived." Faith was running high as Christians gathered to flaunt their numbers at massive rallies, festivals, and conventions. Christians were everywhere. From the locker rooms of the Cincinnati Reds and Dallas Cowboys to corporate executive offices. From glittering Hollywood to the White House. Revival had come!

In recent days, however, I have become increasingly aware that all is not well . . . that something is missing.

Is it possible that some of us have extended a flawed lifeline? Can it be that in our harvest zeal we have actually offered a substitute gospel? Oliver Cromwell, the great English states-

11

man and military leader, remarked, "No one rises so high as he who knows not whither he is going."

The Spirit of the Lord is steadfastly drawing me to a more honest comparison of the characteristics of our revival with those recorded in His Word and recent history. Some very serious questions have seemingly gathered around me with raised eyebrows. Why, for instance, if there are 40-50 million truly born-again Christians in this country, can't we impress God's stamp of holiness on our nation? Why is the fabric of society coming apart at the seams? Let's face it—in every major area of national endeavor, be it political, legal, or educational, we are witnessing rapid moral decline. This phenomenon is not consistent with the social influence of the past revivals. When we take an honest look at the heart of America we can only see grave wounds. Our woes flow directly from our trend toward a former bankrupt generation when "everyone did that which seemed good in his own eyes."

We must beware lest our highly organized, media-oriented, spiritual juggernauts produce converts like the tin man in the Wizard of Oz—minus a heart.

I believe if there is to be a reversal of the humanistic trend toward self-indulgent moral intoxication, we absolutely must change our approach. The high-gloss Madison Avenue thrust must be replaced with the Calvary approach—painful but lasting, lowly but victorious.

What is wrong? What is the missing ingredient in this morally lethargic religious Behemoth posing as revival? The answer lies buried within the heart of one word—*Holiness.* "For God hath not called us unto uncleanness, but unto holiness." Here is the focus of God's attention—and let me state this is where it has always been. The message of this book is not a new one. It is a cry that has been sounded down through the centuries. But it needs to be sounded again—for Satan can never grip a people or a land where believers are willing to pay the price of spiritual purity to liberate them.

1
Roots

Bang the drum slowly, the revival is dying. Its roots are matted and shallow. Its leaves are withering in the firestorm of today's sin. And like a plant cut off at the roots, the revival's flower is an illusion blooming: its petals soon to drop...

Our prosperity is an anesthetic—it's all about us, the deadening effects of material well-being hiding an internal cancer of sin and bankruptcy within our nation. The flood of evangelical literature, Christian meetings, and religious television help obscure (especially from Christians) the slow death that is taking place as the result of the fumes of moral corruption throughout the land.

Has God written "Ichabod" across the nation? And who is to blame? Sinners? Or maybe even the saints themselves?

Every member of God's household will be held accountable. Yet, I suspect, from God's perspective, He may hold spiritual leaders the most responsible. We have not been bold watchmen, nor vocal shepherds. How willingly we proclaim the good news of salvation, grace, peace, prosperity, love and miracles, as if this was the whole story! Many of us have become unbalanced shepherds.

They have healed also the hurt of the daughter of my

people slightly, saying, Peace, peace; when there is no peace...therefore they shall fall among them that fall....[1]

We have failed to arouse the fear of God amongst the people in our land. We see anxious people streaming forward to receive prayer for the healing of their infirmities or for miscellaneous blessings. How often, though, have we called our people forward in order to pray for a fresh desire for obedience, and, for a new fear of the Lord?

How dare we, who are charged as His ministers, hesitate to proclaim whatsoever His Spirit wants because we assume the people might not like it? Are we spiritual entertainers desiring the praises and support of men more than obedience to, and approval, of God?

The prophets prophesy falsely, and the priests bear rule by their means; and my people love to have it so: and what will ye do in the end thereof?[2]

People with cold hearts love religious "sugar" more than a true word from God.

No subject is more frequently mentioned in the Bible than the holiness of God and His continuous call for a pure, righteous, and holy family. May God forgive us for our failure to give this exciting theme the same priority given by our Lord. No wonder our roots run so shallow. We have been growing in fallow ground, caked hard for lack of those conscience-quickening plows. How desperately we need moral nourishment—for survival.

Early Thoughts on Righteousness

As a nation we are following the very path one man of vision feared we might take. Thomas Jefferson said, wondering about the country's future, "Yes, we did produce a near perfect Republic. But will they keep it, or will they in the enjoyment of

14

plenty, lose the memory of freedom? Material abundance without character is the surest way to destruction."

Another American prophet-of-the-past also spoke his concern. Daniel Webster warned: "If the power of the Gospel is not felt throughout the length and breadth of the land, then anarchy and misrule, degradation and misery, corruption and darkness will reign without mitigation. . . . If God and His Word are not known and received, then the devil and his works will gain ascendancy. . . . If the evangelical volume does not reach every hamlet, then the pages of a corrupt and licentious literature will. . . . If courageous and religious books are not widely circulated in this country, I do not know what is to become of us as a nation. The Bible is our safe guide; so long as we take it as our instructor and follow it for conduct and character, we will go on prospering in the future. But the moment we relegate its influence from our lives a catastrophe will come to us such as we have never known."

Abraham Lincoln, while President, wasn't ashamed to acknowledge God, "I believe in His eternal truth and justice and that God's will must prevail. Without Him, all human reliance is in vain: Without the assistance of the Divine Being I cannot succeed: With that assistance I cannot fail. I desire that all my works and acts may be according to His will."

Such was the leadership of our rising young country.

Deep spiritual roots grew rapidly then, because the leaders established government on a solid moral base. The result was a meteoric rise to global prominence. Why? Because a spiritual law was being fulfilled: "Righteousness exalteth a nation . . . "[3]

In time, however, deterioration set in; the early roots-of-righteousness were neglected. The young republic began to flounder. The weeds of greed and selfishness started to sprout, and brought with them the blight of slavery. The nation convulsed and nearly died altogether, fighting its bloodiest test of survival, the Civil War.

America did not perish. Good roots once again began

15

working their way down into her heart. Under the ministry of Charles G. Finney the fallow ground of the nation was broken up and righteousness prevailed. The country was refreshened and took on beauty, productivity, and strength, and the people sang:

O beautiful for pilgrim feet,
Whose stern impassioned stress
A thoroughfare for freedom beat
Across the wilderness.
America! America!
God mend thine every flaw,
Confirm thy soul in self control,
Thy liberty in law!

. . . .
America! America!
May God thy gold refine
Till all success be nobleness,
And every gain Divine!

The industrial, technological, and scientific revolution which followed soon established America at the pinnacle of nations. But as time passed, humility and hard work gave way to indulgent sophistication and, once again, the country drifted downward. Prayer and the Bible were ruled out of schoolrooms and the "new morality" took root. A fulfillment of Daniel Webster's greatest fear: ". . . the moment we relegate righteousness from our lives a catastrophe will come of a dimension we have never known."

We are still reeling. Our most recent set of woes, inflation/recession, rising crime, high-level corruption, and military defeat have conclusively exposed our dying roots. The fear of God and its attendant wisdom have all but vanished, and our great nation has become a staggering, despised giant, a classic example of "distress and perplexity of nations."[4]

Long ago a nation like ours drifted into iniquity, confusion, and spiritual neglect. So much so that its sanctuary had filled up with rubble and debris. Yet even in that hopeless condition,

16

an answer was discovered. It wasn't a new answer, but an old one, and just what the troubled nation needed. The Scrolls of the Word were found in the rubble of the sanctuary. They had been there all the time. The finder ran to the king.

That king was wise. Recognizing the value of the discovery he immediately sent his carpenters scurrying to build a high wooden platform. He then called all the people together, and the Word of God was read from the high stage. How did the people react? They stood for hours, day after day, drinking in the Word, and then they cheered, clapped, and praised God until the noise of their excitement could be heard for miles! [5]

If My People

I was working at my desk one morning when God seared a Scripture on my mind with smoking intensity. It was (the now familiar) II Chronicles 7:14: "If my people, which are called by my name, shall humble themselves, and pray, and seek my face, and turn from their wicked ways; then will I hear from heaven, and forgive their sin, and will heal their land."

If my people . . .

It rang with such power and hope! I began to herald it across the land, in meetings, on television, and in a book, *Crisis America*. It seemed to me the verse was like a telegraphic promise from God to a people desperately in need of healing. Americans leaped at the promise from Chronicles. It seemed our country was again on its way to revival. We began to pray and fast, for both the country and our leaders. Faith was running at a new high.

What happened? Everyone knows America was never healed. In fact, she grew sicker than ever.

With every Divine promise there is also a condition. The promise for the healing of the country in II Chronicles 7:14 hinged on the condition that Christians—"those who are called by my name"—turn from their wicked ways. We never did it!

17

God was calling His people to return to righteousness so that He might heal the land. Sin in America, and within the Body of Christ, *increased* rather than abated. No wonder the crises and problems grew.

Has worldly sophistication, permissiveness, and compromise taken such deep root? Are they ineradicable? Are we as spiritual shepherds afraid to speak out against sin in the Body, because we fear for our popularity or face smaller collection-plate offerings? Do we fear driving some from our meetings? How much safer to schedule a musical, a miracle meeting, a prosperity-selling evangelist—or Bingo!

> But you shall speak My words to them whether they listen or not, for they are rebellious.[6]

2
The Sky Is Falling

No danger threatens the dynamic of this nation more than the quenching of its revival, and a threat does exist, for there are many signs.

This nation's greatest revivalist was the lawyer-turned-preacher, Charles Grandison Finney, who led the great American revival during the mid-1800s. He emphasized God's expectations with regard to active opposition to immoral national trends. Once he cautioned his audience that their revival showed signs of lagging, and then documented his case with 14 points of evidence, thundering at his summation, "The church must testify to the truth, the whole truth, and nothing but the truth on this subject, or else."

God is always in a state of revival. *Moves of God are never halted by His edict, but rather by the mandate of His people.* The only way to preserve the present move of God is to face up, however painful it may be, to the fact that it really is showing signs of deteriorating. Prayerful examination never hurts a revival, but there must be a willingness to let the Holy Spirit reveal danger symptoms. Only then can we take victorious countermeasures. Jesus often spoke in unvarnished language when He perceived spiritual danger among the people. Some today might criticize Jesus' behavior as negative, unloving, and judgmental. But His love, because it was pure, dealt with reality. Addressing the most respected and proud churchmen of His day, Jesus called them, "Whited sepulchers full of dead men's bones . . . blind guides leading the blind."[1] Jesus pulled the cover off sin and complacency. Refusing to be drawn into a popularity contest, He sought ways to operate consistently in the character of His heavenly Father.

Oh, pray for straight-talking prophets to be raised up in the land before it is too late! That we might hear them out and not stone them to silence.

Spiritual Gypsies

An interesting thing happened recently at a Christian convention where I was one of the teachers. Between sessions, I was approached by a retired couple eager to share about the new lifestyle God had "led them into." Leading me out into the parking lot they proudly pointed to an elegant motorhome. They proceeded to share how they were criss-crossing the country, gloriously consuming Christian meetings, seminars and conventions.

I couldn't share their enthusiasm . . . but it was nonetheless an enlightening encounter. And I might add it is becoming more typical every day to encounter spiritual gypsies running from one meeting to the next. Instead of waiting on God for revelation themselves, they seek vicarious thrills through listening to the victory testimony of others.

Then there are the armchair Christians. They do their roving the same way through Christian television. They sit glued to their sets for hours on end, using the songs, testimonies, and Scriptures almost like tranquilizers. The Bible warns that we are not to be simply hearers of the Word, but *doers* also!

Some have become miracle chasers, unwilling to make the hard choices necessary for righteous living in the secret of their hearts . . . unwilling to grow where they are planted.

There are, today, many forms of "spiritual entertainment," but this can never be substituted for the lofty but often lonely walk of true discipleship.

Fellowship can be edifying. We feel safe, so peaceful, so satisfied in the midst of hundreds of hymn-singing Christians. And yet togetherness can produce a soulish brand of peace, even a spiritual smugness.

God is crying today, "Oh, when will you be willing to pay the price for victory and power in your own life? Why are you so eager to seek power through others and so unwilling to seek Me directly?"

The State of the Nation

If there is a stench which God really abhors, it is the lack of concern over sin among His own people. Many Christians have all but adjusted to the moral situation around them. Sin is not their concern, there is nothing they can do about it. Is that your attitude? Others accept it as a sign of the coming rapture. God, however, has made it unmistakably clear that He holds us accountable. We are to "occupy" until Christ comes.

Perversion is becoming so acceptable that five homosexual leaders were received at the White House itself recently. Jody Powell, the President's press secretary, commenting on their meeting: "Now this is what America is all about." Many state laws have now legalized this sin which is so repugnant to God.

The nation's pornography or "flesh industry" grosses $17 billion annually. It has set aflame such passions that rape and sexual murders have skyrocketed. Perverted passions are responsible for one million cases of child abuse annually. And, what's more, we are told that only about one out of every four cases are being reported.

The drug explosion is another blight on the U.S. More Americans are dying now from drugs than were killed in the

21

Vietnam war. Alcohol has proven even more devastating. Not only are there more than 100,000 children from seven to ten years of age who are confirmed alcoholics, but *America is now losing $32 billion every year thanks to the liquor industry.* How much longer can God stay His hand of judgment? How much longer indeed, when the very stream of life itself is interrupted in two million murders in the slaughter of innocent, helpless infants nestled in the "safety" of their mothers' wombs?

And we now face the pale specter of genetic engineering. Scientists tinkering with the chromosomes ... God's secret blueprints for life. Throughout human history God has protected the integrity and continuity of life by making certain through the chromosomes that life would bring forth life after its own kind. Now we hear ominous bragging from the laboratories of the potential to hybridize the stream of life. The grim joke is "making trees bark and dogs to grow leaves."

Consider Ezekiel's chilling message to the nation. It came on a day when the Lord's grief over proliferating sin in the Holy City of Jerusalem reached a breaking point—a day, I am convinced, which we are rapidly approaching once again.

Suddenly, we are told, the Spirit of the Lord spoke out from the wall of the great sanctuary in Jerusalem:

> Cause them that have charge over the city to draw near, even every man with his destroying weapon in his hand. And, behold, six men came from the way of the higher gate, which lieth toward the north, and every man a slaughter weapon in his hand; and one man among them was clothed with linen, with a writer's inkhorn by his side: and they went in, and stood beside the bronze altar. And the glory of the God of Israel was gone up from the cherub whereupon he was, to the threshold of the house.[2]

The words reverberate down the centuries: *destroying weapon, slaughter weapon.* Sin is to be dealt with sharply, cleanly, and absolutely.

Ezekiel's account of what happened continues:

And he called to the man clothed with linen, which had the writer's inkhorn by his side; and the Lord said unto him, Go through the midst of the city, through the midst of Jerusalem, and set a *mark* upon the foreheads of the men that sigh and that cry for all the abominations that be done in the midst thereof. And to the others he said in mine hearing, Go ye after him through the city, and smite: let not your eye spare, neither have ye pity: slay utterly . . . but come not near any man upon whom is the mark . . . [3]

After the Lord had sent His messengers through the Holy City to mark the foreheads of each who was troubled and distressed over the growing sin and unholiness in the city, God spoke these ominous words to the destroyers, "AND BEGIN AT MY SANCTUARY!"

Why do you think God looked first to the sanctuary? Let me put it this way: Have you ever had the misfortune of seeing an acquaintance, vigorous-looking and rosy-cheeked, only to learn a short time later that a doctor's routine examination revealed he was riddled with cancer? That is the picture of the sanctuary God is speaking of. Beautiful building, fine music, large audience. On the surface beautiful, but morally weak and spiritually impotent to correct the nation's sin. He marked the foreheads of those who are concerned and who will restore the sanctuary. Will He mark our foreheads? Are there foreheads to be marked?

No revival in history has had "staying power" unless purity, holiness, righteousness were burned into the minds and hearts of the listeners. Our revival lags today. It is big, spectacular, and it cuts a wide swath of converts. For this we rejoice. Still, there is something missing.

The point is that our moral sky is falling! Chicken Little's warning was a fairy tale. Unfortunately, today's warning is reality. And we can't, like Scarlet O'Hara, brush it off day after day,

23

saying, "I'll think about it tomorrow." Tomorrow is here, and we must get about our Father's business. We don't need Charles Finney to document 14 points of evidence that our moral sky is falling. Chunks of our failing morality hit our consciences every day—what isn't directly in sight is reported by radio, TV, news magazines and newspapers—there's no getting away from SIN.

In a past crisis, God sought for a man who would stand in the gap to save the land. How shocking that none could be found! Will He find one this time?

3

The Thunder of God

"By the word of His mouth everything is held together." [1]

The microcosms of swarming atomic worlds obediently congealed to form matter when God spoke the worlds into being. His spirit established the proper locale for each star and planet, then with the breath from His mouth, sent our universe spinning into motion. For thousands of years man has been awed by the cosmic signature of God whenever he has glanced upward. David was impressed, "When I consider thy heavens, the work of thy fingers, the moon and the stars, which thou hast ordained; what is man, that thou art mindful of him?" [2]

Equally dazzled are those who have discovered this same living God has been working on a blueprint which includes them as "partners"—joint heirs to all this power and real estate.

In other words, design believers are wired right into the power of heaven itself. And if that power is not flowing in any life it is because the "power lines" from the hill of God have been damaged by an absence of faith and presence of sin. God asks, "Who shall ascend into the hill of the Lord?" [3] He then gives the answer, "He that hath clean hands, and a pure heart. . . . " [4] The power of God has never diminished, nor has He denied His people the freedom to tap that power—so long

25

as they exercise faith and comply with His spiritual rules!

Releasing the Flow of God's Power

Oh, for a faith that will not shrink
Tho' pressed by every foe,
That will not tremble on the brink
Of any earthly woe!

That will not murmur nor complain
Beneath the chastening rod,
But in the hour of grief or pain
Will lean upon its God.

A faith that shines more bright and clear
When tempests rage without,
That when in danger knows no fear
In darkness feels no doubt.

—William Bath

Yes, faith is the switch we must throw to energize that spiritual voltage of heaven. The Bible says, by faith, Noah, being warned of God of things not seen as yet, prepared an ark to the saving of his house. And Abraham was called a friend because "he staggered not at the promise" of God.

Through faith also Sarah herself received strength to conceive seed, and was delivered of a child when she was past age.... "Therefore sprang there even of one, and him as good as dead, so many as the stars of the sky in multitude.... By faith they passed through the Red sea as by dry land.... By faith the walls of Jericho fell down.... Through faith subdued kingdoms, wrought righteousness, obtained promises, stopped the mouths of lions, quenched the violence of fire, escaped the edge of the sword, out of weakness were made strong, waxed valiant in fight, turned to flight the armies of the aliens. Women received their dead raised to life again." [5]

While faith truly is the switch that taps into Divine power, those who understand power distribution know that a switch without a good wire to bring current from the power source is useless.

Many years ago I worked for the Belden Wire & Cable Company. Expensive and elaborate technology was employed to remove the impurities from copper wire to insure that it would effectively transmit electric current. If impurities were not removed from the raw copper, these impurities restricted the wire's ability to conduct the amount of power it was designed to carry. So it is with the Body of Christ today. Our potential to be conductors of God's power is often restricted by impurities in our lives. I am persuaded this is why we can, at times, "whomp up" such a soulish enthusiasm that a meeting seems electric, and yet the ultimate results are little more than the harmless "pop" of static electricity. No eternal changes and spiritual growth result from many such meetings—we pay too little attention to purging our impurities.

God speaks of removing dross from gold (the purer the gold, the higher its karat value). Glass becomes clearer when it is subjected to the furnaces of purification. Filters are utilized to eliminate impurities so engines can develop full power.

When we have been experiencing restriction in our performance, ask the Lord to reveal impurities which may be reducing our own spiritual power. Purity and holiness are never subordinate with the Lord, "with whom is no variableness, neither shadow of turning." [6] There's never a hint of God lowering His moral standards to fit the conditions of society.

We are hearing a lot nowadays about "super faith" teachers. Thank God for them. Perhaps we should now pray for the raising up of "super holiness" teachers, that better balance might be attained in the Body.

The Bible, God's book of memorable deeds, cites many examples of supernatural power manifested when, in generations past, righteous men exercised faith. We read, "Then all the multitude kept silence, and gave audience to Barnabas and Paul, declaring what miracles and wonders God had wrought . . . by them." [7] And it is there that our spiritual dynamic (faith) is increased by remembering the mighty works of God.

27

Rarely if ever in our day do we see *every* sick person at a meeting leave healed. It is always exciting to see even a dozen healed in meetings today. When Jesus ministered, "He healed them all." Nor are we seeing the corpse rise up from death like Jesus ministered to Lazarus.

"Wait just a minute," you say, "that's not a fair comparison. Jesus was God."

Yes, it is worthy of comparison because Jesus came to be our example, to show us the Kingdom of God in action. When the power of Heaven worked through Him, bringing about miracles, He was operating as the "Son of Man." Jesus Himself said, "Greater works shall you do." [8]

Then how did Jesus accomplish His mighty deeds? He *knew* the spiritual power available. He desired to do the will of the Father and always operated within the master blueprint as outlined in God's Word. A dominant secret of Jesus' power lay in the purity of His life. There were no sinful impurities restricting the full voltage of Heaven from flowing freely through Him! It was Jesus' holiness and His obedience so perfectly harmonizing with the Father which enabled Him to manifest such awesome power. Now remember, "Greater works shall you do." He came to show *us* how to do those greater works. But we aren't really seeing the greater works until we embrace holiness as well as faith.

Those first-century Christians, moving in cadence to Jesus' own holy steps, generated a spiritual atmosphere in which the manifested power of God was the norm. Earthquakes jarred open jail doors! Philip flew through the air, dispatched by the Spirit to *intersect* a chariot in the desert! Three thousand decisions were made for Christ at the first sermon of an illiterate fisherman! People dragged their sick out to the street expecting the shadow of one Christian to bring about a miracle healing! The Word of God declares these book of Acts Christians, functioning in faith and righteousness, "turned the world upside down."

28

I recently stood in ancient Ephesus marveling at the size of that metropolis to which Paul brought such consternation. It is the site of one of the seven wonders of the ancient world, the Temple of Diana of the Ephesians from which Paul courageously thundered truth about the only Son of God. His message and ministry of deliverance shattered the demonic traditions of that community to such an extent that Ephesian idol makers were tearing their hair out. A riot broke out in Ephesus because the moral status quo was shattered by the apostle's power.

Why are the sick never maneuvered or helped today to be crossed over by shadows? Why are sin cities hardly fazed today by our entrance? The people of Mars Hill, Corinth, and Ephesus were "shook up" and painfully conscious that Paul had entered their city.

When I compare my own spiritual power with many of the Bible heroes, it is so much weaker. But I cannot rationalize away my lesser spiritual power because God said, "He is no respecter of persons." He doesn't have favorites. God is as ready to manifest His power through any faith-charged, righteous believer today.

Our nation is now facing the most powerful armed enemy in history. The United States stands in need of the thunder of God's power to survive and that power is available if believers will utilize it. J. Edgar Hoover once said, "The spiritual firepower of the Christian church, based on the love of God, is sufficient to destroy all the Soviet man-made missiles and rockets, and the Communists know it and fear it."

My hope is that our generation may be provoked to jealousy as we recognize how much more Acts believers accomplished. May we grow dissatisfied with anything less than a Joshua-level of relationship with our Lord which can stop the sun when necessary. Dissatisfied until we see a greater thirsting for righteousness—dissatisfied until we become conduits through which His power can surge to new heights for the salvation of our generation. Oh, how we could benefit from a Spirit-prompted dissatisfaction with our present spirituality. Jesus said, "Blessed are they which do hunger and thirst after righteousness: for they shall be filled." [9]

Harald Bredesen once shouted words that still ricochet through my soul, "The heart of God is more grieved by the satisfiedness of the saints than by the wickedness of the sinners!"

So, let us be very thankful for what God is doing today, but willing to pay any price to achieve the higher maximum He intended. We need a revival within the revival. Every past revival has died out through a slow increase of the unrighteousness in the Body brought on by complacency.

But history shows us several dying revivals which were sparked again when the saints recognized the warning and took corrective spiritual action. I am convinced this revival will also respond.

4
The Finney Formula

Truth is not only stranger than fiction but vastly more exciting. People in our day seem hooked on fiction and bizarre plots, thereby fulfilling a prophecy which further identifies this generation as being in the end time: "They shall turn away their ears from the truth, and shall be turned unto fables." [1]

The eyes and ears of America are fixed on soap operas, cartoons, and hour after boring hour of TV stories. Sex, outlandishness, and foul language are substituted for creativity.

But these cheap Hollywood thrills pale before the grand script of reality. One of my favorites is a real-life plot from Jewish history which carries its own surprise ending. Some 470 years before Christ, a powerful king reigned in Persia. His name was Xerxes (his Bible name is Ahasuerus). This marauding conqueror had captured the whole Jewish nation, including a strikingly beautiful young woman, Esther, and her devout cousin, Mordecai. The people of God were imperiled from having to live as sojourners in the midst of a wicked nation (not unlike many Christians today). A clever and powerful villain by the name of Haman soon appeared. He set in motion a complex plan to destroy all the Jews.

Meanwhile, back in a domestic wing of the palace, things

31

were growing tense between King Xerxes and his queen, Vashti. King Xerxes finally divorced Vashti for her refusal to be submissive, and began the search for a new bride. What happened next is one of the most romantic stories of history. Would you believe that our beautiful Jewish heroine, Esther, ended up as King Xerxes' queen? Well, she did.

When our snarling villain, Haman, erected a great big scaffold to hang Esther's God-honoring cousin, Mordecai, the intrigue quickened. But, when the dust finally settled, there hung villain Haman on the very scaffold he had erected for cousin Mordecai. The hero lived while the villain Haman twirled slowly in the sun. Mordecai, during the course of the Jews' darkest outlook, called upon Queen Esther to risk her life by revealing to her husband, King Ahasuerus, that she was a Jewess and to plead for them to be spared. Mordecai said, "Perhaps God raised you up for such a time as this!"

As a result of Queen Esther's bold intercession, both cousin Mordecai and the Jews were showered with unexpected honors and blessings by the powerful king of the Medes and Persians. To this very day in Israel, celebration of this victorious ending is observed. Remembrance of God's deliverance through Queen Esther is celebrated, complete with miniature "Haman's gallows."

Our generation has a host of both national perils to threaten it and spiritual opportunities to help it—perhaps you were raised up by God for such a time as this? We are at a time when our own government and its leaders have grown dizzy with power. Spokesmen of principles, the Daniel Websters, have all but vanished from the land. They borrow from our children's future by deficit spending. "The prosperity of the land is in her righteousness."

These same politicians are "reforming" the moral, Bible-based laws of the land. While the President likes to say that his administration is bringing about a revolution of enactments, it is well to remember that change doesn't always mean improvement.

Our so-called liberal leaders have ruled in favor of decriminalizing drug use and terminating the lives of unwanted infants while banning God from the schools. If that weren't enough, they have affixed their stamp of approval on pornography and perversion. They have comforted the criminal and hissed at his victim, fostering an environment for God's people similar to that faced by the Jews in the Persian Empire.

What today stands out in Esther's story are Mordecai's words to the young girl suddenly elevated to queen: "And who knoweth whether thou art come to the kingdom for such a time as this?" [2] At great peril to herself, Esther seized her opportunity to effect a triumphant delivery for her people.

It seems just about as hopeless for Christians today as it must have seemed to Esther. If, however, Christians arise to their potential through God, as did Mordecai and Esther, the United States will be in for some happy surprises too.

But, some may say, "There are too few of us who really care about righteousness, and too many of those who love the 'moral freedoms' in this society."

But don't forget Mordecai and Esther. Don't forget the 12 who poured out of the Upper Room and turned the world "upside down." Don't forget John Wesley who, in the late 1700s, commenced a revival that reshaped the entire British nation. John Wesley's work was distinguished by its heavy emphasis on holiness. The Wesleyan revival was unique in that during the entire course of his ministry, only two to three percent of the population of England received Christ. Insignificant in the quantity of its harvest, but dynamite in the quality of its converts and the results!

Wesley's disciples, through their combination of purity and faith, demonstrated again that a remnant plus God can turn a whole nation.

With all the emphasis on spiritual power in this big revival today we have not impressed a moral stamp on the nation. In contrast, Wesley's totally consecrated minority effected the posting of "out of business" notices on six out of seven English taverns. This tiny group's impact was so profound that much of the highly revered English law was recast under their influence to conform their principles to the Bible. It is most distressing that the 40 to 50 million professed "born again" Christians cannot slow the flood of moral pollution, wickedness, and corruption in our nation. That says something, and maybe it is time to emphasize quality and de-emphasize quantity.

Sometimes redundancy can bring a sharper emphasis. Our "revival" is weak. Some say it is sick. We need to cry out to God for mercy, as did Isaiah crying, "Woe is me! for I am undone; because I am a man of unclean lips, and I dwell in the midst of a people of unclean lips: for mine eyes have seen the King, the Lord of hosts." [3]

The only revival in America's history which had real staying power was that connected with Evangelist Charles G. Finney. Every single day for 30 years its dominant theme was repeated: holiness, sanctification, responsibility. *That* revival had guts; it changed the lives of millions and the character of the nation itself.

When our young people have to dust off the tedious but potent books of old Charles Finney in their hunger for the real thing, it ought to signal the teachers and writers of today. They are ready to include the holiness component of the revival.

If some bearing the name of Christian (Little Christs) are offering only a qualified commitment, then it behooves them to change their ways. Nothing is more confusing to the unsaved than observing Christians behaving just like the world.

Alexander the Great led a disciplined and therefore victorious military machine. When it came to insubordination and willful mental incompetence, he permitted little or no margin of tolerance.

Late one night, as the Greek army was relaxing from a series of battles, Alexander decided to cure his insomnia by making a surprise check of the sentry posts guarding the camp. Any sentry caught sleeping was to be automatically executed. This was due to the fact that a sleeping guard endangered the lives of thousands at a time when they were most vulnerable—asleep and unprepared for battle. Near the end of Alexander's inspection he encountered a young sentry fast asleep. Alexander demanded the young sentry's name. Upon hearing that his name was Alexander too, the general replied, "Soldier, change your conduct or change your name!"

The Bible says our lives are a spectacle before men and angels. What kind of spectacle are we setting who are known to bear His name? Remember John Knox, of whom Mary, queen of the Scots, said, "I more fear the prayers of a John Knox than all the armies of France!" What kind of reputation are we living before our neighbors and those with whom we come in contact?

Maybe some ought to sing a modified version of the old hymn, "I Surrender All." Perhaps something like, "I surrender all but my bank account, my business, my family, etc. . . . " In Revelation, the Spirit of God warned the Laodicean Christians to make up their minds speedily, to fish or cut bait, when the Spirit said, in effect, "Get either hot or cold. If you remain lukewarm, I'll spit you out." [4]

I'll tell you this, those prophets in former generations knew how to meet spiritual vacillation. They looked the people straight in the eye and demanded commitment, shouting, "How long will you hesitate between two opinions? If the Lord is God, follow Him; but if Baal, follow him." [5]

In so much of our preaching today there is an implied promise that Christians can have God's rich blessings right along with all their secular "fun."

But Jesus taught, "Where your treasure is, there will your heart be." [6] Where your treasure, or the investment of your life, is focused, you will be pulled like a magnet. Choose treasure in heaven (spiritual wealth) or pleasures and treasures on this earth, which inevitably will perish. Take the example of the rich fool. He loved his treasure. And like so many today who would be "masters of their fate, captains of their souls," he said to himself, "I will tear down my barns and build bigger ones, and then eat, live and be merry." He promptly died and departed for a place where he couldn't take a penny of his treasure! [7] The rich fool had qualified his commitment.

Jesus did indeed use material things, even had need for them as you and I—but He kept them subordinate to His purpose. He was not dominated by them.

Today's generation needs a refreshening calling forth to Him—a strong charge of the fear of the Lord—in the real sense, to be born again. There is desperate need for a revival within this revival. And God is ready to back it with all the resources of Heaven!

5
Revival or Ashes

Striking are the parallels in conditions which prevailed just before Rome collapsed with those prevailing today in America. So, drawing from the archives of history, let us examine the setting in which the world's most powerful empire failed. The ashes of the Caesars still speak to those who want to learn. Comparisons are chilling if you substitute *U.S.* for *Rome* in the following listing of status of the Roman society.

- Roman bureaucracy grew ever more humanistic in the conviction that man and his programs could solve all problems.
- A flurry of legal "reforms" and huge welfare programs were enacted.
- When gross immorality and violence flourished, Roman laws were liberalized to accommodate the downward drift in society.
- Self-interest began to dominate society as a whole. Statesmanship vanished. Politicians enacted programs which would please the people in order to keep themselves in power. Political moves were designed for immediate benefits regardless of deteriorating effects they would bring upon future generations.

- Cruelty grew epidemic among its citizens. Their appetite increased for more sensual experiences. When this sensuality wasn't discouraged by the government, it was manifest in blatant homosexuality, pornography, sexual orgies, and bloody human contests in the Colosseum. (If it feels good, do it.) A libertine atmosphere prevailed.
- Unbridled "human rights" became a link in Rome's chain to destruction.
- When civil strife increased, the government grew more authoritarian and a widening gulf developed between the governors and the governed. The bureaucracy became obsessed with methods to retain their governing positions at any cost.
- Many new gods and new religions sprang up.
- Toward the end, the Roman governors no longer cared who or how the people worshipped so long as the government remained preeminent.
- The Christians were persecuted for speaking out against the government and for refusal to worship Caesar.
- Roman music grew increasingly bombastic.
- The quality of the arts diminished.
- Treason and corruption broke out among upper echelon politicians.
- Debauchery extended all the way up to Caesar's palace.
- The government grew cumbersome and very costly.
- When Roman taxes crushed incentive, production dropped and inflation staggered the economy.
- Patriotism among the populace vanished along with respect for the government.
- Military valor diminished and the will to defend the empire prepared the way for outside attacks.
- The last straw was apathy. People gave up hope of ever being able to influence the course of their government.
- Anarchy broke out.
- The collapse of the Roman Empire reverberated

throughout the whole world and brought political and social chaos far and wide.

The great Roman orator, Marcus Cicero, arose one day before the Roman Senate and said:

> We are taxed in our bread and in our wine, in our incomes and our investments, on our land and on our property, not only for base creatures who do not deserve the name of man, but for foreign nations, for complacent nations who will bow to us and accept our largesse and promise to assist us in the keeping of peace—these mendicant nations who will destroy us when we show a moment of weakness when our treasury is bare, and surely it is becoming bare. We are taxed to maintain legions on their soil. . . . We keep them in precarious balance only with our gold. . . . They take our very flesh and they hate and despise us.

Moral and political similarities in Rome just before its collapse and conditions with those in the United States today are sobering. Moral disintegration again threatens a great ship of state. Only the power from an intensified revival can save her. The survival of the United States as a nation is dependent upon such a moral revival—and God will back it! May we again hear revival bells ringing in America from sea to shining sea.

We should desire to see this nation live, not just to preserve its democratic system or just because it is our home. The primary motivation should be an obedience to God's injunction, "Occupy until I come." The salvation of America is essential to preserve her as a revival base to spread the gospel.

If America's freedom should be extinguished through our neglect the revival she now harbors would likewise be extinguished. May we pray and work to prevent history repeating. Only the children of God have the power to seize the horn of history and snatch victory from the present moral wreckage.

In the world's broad field of battle,
In the bivouac of life,
Be not like dumb, driven cattle!

39

Be a hero in the strife!
Act, —act in the living present!
Heart within, and God o'er head!
                    —Henry Wadsworth Longfellow

6

The Dynamic of Commitment

There is hardly a Christian who hasn't marveled at the things God is doing. The level of satisfaction in the scope of this present revival seems close to an all-time high. We justifiably thrill that every major city is now covered by Christian radio and television. We cheer the statistics of church and "Sunday School" attendance and take pride at the pollsters' findings of "born again" might.

The Bible speaks of similar bustling activities and soaring statistics in the seven churches of the Revelation.

> And to the angel of the church in Laodicea write: . . . I know your deeds. . . . you are neither cold nor hot. So because you are lukewarm, and neither cold nor hot, I will spit you out of My mouth! For you say, "I am rich, I have prospered, and I need nothing"; not knowing you are wretched, pitiably . . . but I have something against thee.[1]

It grieves God when there is less than total commitment to advancing His Kingdom. A dual allegiance to the things of this world and the things of God is plaguing believers. In a former

41

time of muddled allegiance, God hurled this challenge: "Choose you this day whom ye will serve!" [2] Again the Spirit of the Lord is troubled by fickle consecration of many Christians. On Sunday we will sing, "I belong to Jesus"—then on Monday, rejoin the world. Too many want to go with God except when that interferes with their popularity, recreation, or habits.

The secret of the power in the Acts church lay in its consecration. By giving their possessions, energies, and some even their lives, they "turned the world upside down." [3] Total consecration to the Father gave Jesus victory over Satan. Jesus disciplined His every thought, choice, and action to harmonize with the Father: "Not My will but Thine be done." [4] Conversely, partial consecration is the route to misery and failure for any believer.

Today's large spiritual movement is, in some aspects, like the one 300 years after Christ. That revival commenced when a pagan military genius fell on his face when he saw a flaming vision in the sky over central Italy. It occurred during a time when the military might of Rome, lying to the south of him, was to the world invincible. The young military genius from Turkey was named Constantine. He, by then, had already conquered a series of cities and nations, but even Constantine dared not imagine warring against mighty Rome. When he looked into the sky that morning, he was overwhelmed by the sight of a giant flaming sword bearing the inscription, "With this conquer."

Constantine believed that Christ Himself had spoken to him, and that if he were to personally join the cause of Christianity, mighty Rome would be delivered into his hands. He did march on Rome and he won, and, thereafter, he was known as "Constantine the Great." It wasn't long before Constantine and his followers were feverishly responding to this miracle of victory. Constantine proclaimed Christianity the approved religion of his empire.

The impact of Constantine's conversion was felt throughout the entire civilized world. He established his capital in what is now Istanbul, Turkey. The force of his personality was strong and it became "popular" to do what he had done. The fatal weakness of the Constantine brand of "revival" lay in its partial consecration. It comingled the doctrines of Christianity with vestiges of the then-existing heathen worship.

With conversion becoming the expected thing to do, the emperor's followers wasted no time emulating their leader. Entire legions of his troops marched or rode into the waters of Italy's rivers and lakes to participate in mass acts of baptism.

As the soldiers moved into the waters, most raised their right arms clasping swords, holding them out of the water. Constantine's followers consecrated their lives, except for their right arms and the swords which they held back from the baptism. They said, "This (arm and sword) we need to earn our way. This we need to defend ourselves. This we need to fight for Constantine. Everything else we consecrate to the Christian movement."

Constantine's brand of partial commitment to Christ generated mass conversions with shallow spiritual roots. Eventually most "converts" deserted when the next religious bandwagon of Islam rumbled through Turkey.

From Turkey the influence of Constantine's shallow-rooted faith had reached northward into Russia, inspiring the czar's national orthodox church. Its spiritual weakness contributed to the rise of Bolshevism. A huge and lavish cathedral was built back in Istanbul (then Constantinople). It was called St. Sophia's, and suggestively it used a mixture of marble columns from the great Ephesian Temple of the Goddess Diana.

Recently I stood at the center of St. Sophia's in modern Istanbul. As I gazed upward, my eyes were saddened to see the former Christian Church's mosaics mixed with golden Arabic scriptures from the Koran. St. Sophia's is now a Moslem mosque. The failure of Christ's Gospel to take permanent hold in what is now moslem Turkey and atheistic Russia goes back, I am convinced, to the more-than-symbolic unbaptized right arms of Constantine's soldiers. Partial consecration eventually breeds failure in both lives and nations.

"Choose ye this day whom ye will serve. . . . " The Bible says a multiple allegiance is useless because it is shaky and undependable and that "a double-minded man is unstable in all his ways." [5]

The principle of total consecration is repeated countless times throughout Scripture. This truth is inherent in the teachings about a "house divided," in the warnings about being caught up in the things of this world, again in God's exhortation to have "no other gods before Him." [6]

The concept of total commitment is applicable in the natural realm. Every Olympic medalist could relate a story of sacrifice and dedication behind his or her victory. Every successful musician, businessman, or pilot can point to thousands of committed hours spent in pursuit of their goals.

Even skyjackers and terrorists are willing to put their own lives on the line to further causes totally antithetical to the Kingdom of God. Millions of revolutionary Communists have given up homes, families, and freedom in order to taste victory.

A few years ago, the Communists led an uprising in the African nation of Angola. Millions of dollars and hundreds of lives had been invested through American missionary endeavors in Angola. Churches, schools, hospitals, and seminaries were established. But much of the emphasis was focused on education. Little deep commitment to Christ and His gospel was evident. There came a day during that recent revolution when a Communist-indoctrinated rebel squad broke into one Christian classroom. The fiery-eyed revolutionary who led them began to speak to the students. "Come with us; your Christianity will take you nowhere. We have a vision for our country, and we need you to help us. Our dream is a Marxist revolution which will give the power to the people. You can be a part of this vision for Angola and become a part of the victory.

44

But you have to dedicate everything if you come with us. You'll get no pay. You have to steal your own food. We don't even have a gun for you. You must leave your family. It may take years. You'll be hungry, lonely and you may get killed. How many will come and dedicate your lives to fulfilling this great dream?"

We are told that more than half of the students in that Christian school left with the revolutionaries who offered a life of commitment and a goal. How much better if that higher goal of helping to usher in Christ's revolution through total commitment had earlier been instilled.

If we persist in displaying a mere caricature of Christian discipleship, we too are headed toward failure. We will ultimately be finished! Commitment is not optional to winners—it is indispensable. Human beings will commit themselves—and commitment pays dividends no matter what the goal. If we as God's people do not commit ourselves to holiness and aggressive spiritual warfare, then other causes will eventually triumph . . . apocalyptic fatalism notwithstanding.

Some readers, at about this point, may be wondering whether to go on reading this book. We have been so conditional in recent years on "positive thinking" and "positive confession" that the exhortative message may prickle. God, however, spoke regularly through His prophets words of warning and hope because He so loved the world and coveted their safety. So read on, for this book covers not only the problems but the answers to a revitalized revival. The great modern prophet, A. W. Tozer, said, "To be effective the preacher's message must be alive; it must alarm, arouse, challenge; it must be God's present voice to a particular people. It should intrude into the daily and private living of the hearers."

7

Portraits of God

Nothing in this life could be more important than discovering the character of God. To really know the One with whom we will share eternity.

On my barber's wall there is a painting of a little boy on a grassy knoll stooping to pick a tiny flower. The boy's countenance is frozen with fear as an angry and awesome figure looms over the boy shaking a huge finger and mouthing the word "NO!"

I trust this isn't subconsciously your own concept of our God. The Lord of the "Thou shalt nots." One who would squeeze all the fun out of your life. Some Christians shudder when they read about the eyes of the Lord,

"His eyes go to and fro across the earth continually." [1]

"The eyes of the Lord are upon the righteous ..." [2]

He certainly does watch His children but not to find fault and punish as in that ugly painting. Have you ever watched your own little child out of sheer adoration? Well, our Lord is so intimate and loves us so much, He can't keep His eyes off us. God's heart is the most warmly benevolent place in all the universe!

Some time back I was sharing with a group how I had

come to the realization that even the Ten Commandments are whispers of love. The world tends to think of them as fun-stifling restraints from a killjoy God, a God who would erect fences and post "Keep Out" signs in the fun areas of life.

Then it dawned on me that each time my little daughter, Heather, toddled toward a hot burner or toward our swimming pool, I would shout, in effect, "Heather, thou shalt not!" Why did I do this? Was it because I wanted to take all the fun out of her life? Of course not! It was because I loved her so much I didn't want her harmed. I wanted a long, satisfying life for Heather.

That's the way of God's Ten Commandments. Whispers of love from One who desires life and life more abundantly for His own precious children.

> So the Lord commanded us to observe all these stat-
> utes, to fear the Lord our God *for our good always* and
> for our survival, as it is today.[3]

There's something else I don't like about my barber's picture. It portrays God, as men invariably will, as being not only stern, but old and white haired. These attributes emanate from the imaginations of men who have never studied God's "photo album"—the Bible. When we piece together all of the little glimpses that are revealed throughout the Word, quite a lovely picture emerges.

Though God is the Ancient of Days, He is neither senile nor marked by time. He is still the Dayspring, the very essence of vitality. God never slumbers because He's so full of life He doesn't need it. He is life. "... the Lord, the Creator of the ends of the earth, fainteth not, neither is weary..."[4]

A poet, Thomas Sternhold, stretched all his faculties to describe a fleeting glimpse of God.

> The Lord descended from above,
> And bowed the heavens most high,
> And underneath His feet He cast,
> The darkness of the sky.

On cherubim and seraphim
Full royally He rode
And on the wings of mighty wind
Came flying all abroad.

He sat serene upon the floods
Their fury to restrain
And He as sovereign Lord and King
Forevermore shall reign.

A God of incalculable vivaciousness, "Who has measured the waters in the hollow of His hand, and marked off the heavens with the span, and calculated the dust of the earth in the measure, and weighed the mountains in a balance, and the hills in a pair of scales. . . . " [5]

Although He is the Lion of the Tribe of Judah, He is also the Lamb. He is the Almighty, but also the Tender, Intimate One.

My beloved spoke, and said unto me, "Rise up, my love, my fair one, and come away. For lo, the winter is past and the rain is over and gone. The flowers appear on the earth; the time of the singing of the birds has come, and the voice of the turtledove is heard in our land . . . until the day break, and the shadows flee away, I will go up to the mountain of myrrh, and to the hill of frankincense." [6]

Our mighty God shows tenderness and compassion toward those who love the beauty of His holiness.

He hath covered me with the robe of righteousness, as a bridegroom decketh himself with ornaments, and as a bride adorneth herself with her jewels. For as the earth bringeth forth her bud, and as the garden causeth the things that are sown in it to bring forth; so the Lord will cause righteousness and praise to spring forth. . . . [7]

He is the relaxed and gracious Provider found chatting with Adam as they walked through the Garden of Eden in the cool of the day. The One who brought radiance to the face of Moses as he met Him on the mount. The same Moses who had caught the eye of God because of something beautiful 'way down in Moses' heart.

Like many of us today, the children of Israel applauded the mighty WORKS of God which they had personally seen; the miracles of judgment which shook Egypt, the parting of the waters of the Red Sea, manna from heaven, healings from the fiery serpents' bites, and water from the rock. Still they never grew close to God as Moses did. But why? What was Moses' secret? "The children of Israel loved God's *acts*, but Moses loved God's *ways*." [8] The result of the Israelites' pursuit of God's *acts* is revealed in Psalm 106:15: "So He gave them their demands, but sent them leanness in their souls." But as for Moses who loved God's *ways*, "The Lord spake unto Moses face to face, as a man speaketh unto his friend." [9]

He is a good God whom I have come to like as well as love. Do you *like* God? There is a difference between liking and loving. Do you enjoy His ways? Or are you content to witness His *acts*?

At any moment that the ways of our holy God should change, the universe would be doomed. It would take only one big twist of godly inconsistency to set the stars and planets out of their courses. How comforting it is that He is our Father, "with whom is no variableness, neither shadow of turning."[10] Can you grasp the magnificence of His attitude toward sin? The grandeur of His moral stability? We can rejoice that He doesn't change.

How can perfection change but to deteriorate?

International Bible teacher Joy Dawson often talks about "the insanity of sin." If respect for or the fear of God represents the beginning of all *wisdom*, can we see that the opposite— "lack of fear of God"—is insanity? It's a simple matter of concluding, after meditating on who God is, that independence from our Maker is not only undesirable, it is deadly.

If the depth of our relationship with Him hinges on our attitude toward holiness, then it is crucial that we reinstate holiness

50

to the place of prominence God Himself has given it.

Getting the Full Picture

An accurate comprehension of God's character demands that we recognize *all* of His attributes. As beautiful as any single color may be, the rainbow can only be seen when the full spectrum of colors is included. Now it is true that "God is love." But this, like any other truth, when incessantly emphasized to the exclusion of other truths, becomes a distortion. The hearer begins to see God as a narrow-faceted caricature of the real—as weak and impractical. The fear of God diminishes with each syrupy repetition of a love that connotes Divine permissiveness.

The strong emphasis today on the "full gospel" includes the fact that His character consists not only of the component of grace, but equal parts of holiness and justice as well. We need to accept the full range of God's Being, from the tender gentleness of His Spirit epitomized by the dove, to His righteous judgment when He atomized the twin capitals of perversion, Sodom and Gomorrah. Both sin and sinners were dealt with summarily. All that's left of their flourishing world is a deep impression in the earth we call the Dead Sea.

More than once down through history, God has acted when provoked by sin and the defiance in His people's hearts. The same loving God we spoke of all but drowned out humanity to start over again in the days of Noah. Hailstones and fire has He rained down from the skies. Pestilence, drought, and captivity have been His pronouncements upon sin-careless generations.

There are two things Scripture tells us that God takes no pleasure in: Sin and judgment. The one is recorded in the Psalms: "For thou art not a God that hath pleasure *in wickedness*: neither shall evil dwell with thee."[11] The other in Ezekiel: "For I have no pleasure *in the death of him that dieth*, saith the Lord God: wherefore turn yourselves, and live ye."[12]

51

On one hand God declares His revulsion to sin. He exhorts us to hate what He hates. The Psalms go on to say, "The foolish shall not stand in thy sight; thou hatest all workers of iniquity."[13] Then He cries out to us, "Who will rise up for me against evildoers? ... Who will stand up for me against the workers of iniquity?"[14]

It would enrich each of our lives if we would develop a more robust hatred for sin. How wise to replace our tolerance of sin with a passionate revulsion toward it. Unless we develop this hatred for all which God hates, we will continue to lack the motivation to resist sin within ourselves and within our land.

On the other hand, God derives no pleasure from the execution of judgment either. The Scriptures are full of the heart-rending pleadings of a loving God for sinners to put an end to their evil devices so that judgment may be withheld. The climax of God's grief is realized when He knows that all of the means to secure the obedience of a sinner have been exhausted. The abuse of free will by His children has repeatedly put a clamp on the heart of God. Yet when the prodigals of this world repent, they, like the people of Nineveh, will find themselves in the arms of "a gracious and compassionate God, slow to anger and abundant in lovingkindness, and One who relents concerning calamity."[15]

If Only I'd Known Him

The story has been told of a country where a new king had just been crowned. His subjects had never yet seen him. Everyone in a certain village became ecstatic when they learned their new king would pass along the road the next day.

One of his subjects, a beggar, rose early the next morning to take his position along the road. He took along his bowl of rice, the last food he had. As the sun grew hotter and hotter, he anxiously gazed down the long road, hoping that he would spot the royal entourage. The beggar hoped the new king might be a better ruler than the one who ruled during all his past life. At last the new king's party appeared. All the people bowed down, acknowledging his authority over them.

The beggar also bowed as the new king passed. Suddenly he noticed the king's shadow had stopped directly over him. Fearfully, he lifted his eyes. The king descended from his richly adorned stallion and stood right in front of the beggar. The king spoke and his petition surprised the poor beggar, "Son, would you give me of your rice?"

With hesitancy and resentfulness at the king's asking, the beggar reached into his bowl and put several kernels into the king's hand. When the beggar heard the king's party moving on, he looked up to watch the king depart.

Finally, the beggar glanced into his rice bowl and was shocked at what he saw. There was a nugget of gold in place of every single kernel he had shared with his king. In great remorse the beggar cried to himself, "Oh, if only I had really known about my king, I would have given him my all!"

8

The Beauty of Holiness

Give unto the Lord the glory due unto his Name: Bring
an offering, and come before Him: worship the Lord in
the beauty of Holiness.[1]

An amazing discovery in chromosomes was made some
years ago. Medical researchers found that living cells contain a
microscopic "blueprint." This genetic "blueprint," in tiny, un-
formed babies, establishes their coloring, gender, size, and fea-
tures.

Genetic engineering reared the prospect of, sometime in
the future, creating carbon-copy duplicates of human beings.
The process of duplicating cells is called *cloning.* Instead of
growing as a composite from the genes of both a "father" and
"mother," the clone (from the Greek word *klon,* meaning twig
or slip) would be the genetic copy of just one parent.

Although cloning of humans is still far beyond the capabili-
ties of medical science, it remains a fascinating concept. Lippin-
cott recently published a controversial book centering on this
possibility. In the story, *In His Image* (nonfiction!?), an aging,
eccentric millionaire allegedly arranged to have a genetic dupli-
cate of himself created.

But in fact God has, thus far, protected humanity against

this type of self-perpetuation or man-induced immortality. God's policy statement on human immortality during this lifetime was made when His angel drove Adam and Eve away from the Tree of Life.

The very idea of cloning, however, raises an interesting spiritual parallel. God revealed His master design concept for humanity when He declared in Genesis that we are created "in Our image." Now, God was not referring to physical likeness here, but revealing that we are created with the same capability of moral response which He Himself possesses. Unfortunately, man, through sin, broke direct contact from His source (God) and, as a result, lost his moral bearings. The Bible tells us that "God made men upright, but they have sought out many devices."[2]

But God, through His Son Jesus, extended a massive spiritual "cloning" to all those willing to cooperate through becoming born again. What could be more glorious than to become a new creation through this miraculous spiritual process? To become a type of "clone" of Jesus Christ Himself: "For whom He foreknew, He also predestinated to become conformed to the *image of His Son* . . .[3] But we all, with unveiled face beholding as in a mirror the glory of the Lord, are being transformed into the *same image* from glory to glory, just as from the Lord, the Spirit."[4]

We might say the final result of this process will be realized in one rapturous twinkling of an eye, "When we see Him we shall be like Him."

The Word of God puts key emphasis on the development of character. It isn't enough to have "experiences" in the Spirit. We are to cooperate with the Holy Spirit in the building of character. Remember how we have been called to be "conformed to the image of His Son." The New Testament speaks to those who take a certain pride in the fact that they "come behind in no gift" yet fail in the practical duties and virtues, like paying their bills, manifesting a Christian spirit, and generally living as a good example to the unconverted.

A ship with large sails needs a big counterbalance in its keel to prevent it from being blown over by every wind. So it is with those with plenty of experiences and much zeal. The ballast of spiritual virtues listed in the Word is essential to hold them steady and practical. Paul didn't de-Christianize those unstable new converts in Corinth, but he did give "ballast"—the standard of Christian character set forth in the thirteenth chapter of the Epistle written to them. Paul taught them that the victorious Christian life was stabilized by building character, not by just exercising the gifts of the Spirit.

The Beauty of Holiness—Purity

Blessed are the pure in heart: for they shall see God.[5]

The dictionary states that "pure" means clear, free from anything that taints, impairs, or infects. When Jesus talked about the "pure in heart," He had two things in mind. First, of course, He was referring to a heart undefiled; cleaned by repentance and divine forgiveness—and a heart harboring no iniquity. On a deeper level, Jesus was describing an attitude. A right motive or intention of heart in our pursuit of God. A genuine, innocent, and single-minded spiritual enterprise.

Everything in connection with the Tabernacle service in the Old Testament that symbolically pictures the Lord Jesus speaks of purity. The priest's garment, the ceremonial implements, the sacrificial offerings, the fine linen, pure gold, precious stones, costly ointments—all were representative of the character of our Lord Jesus Christ. The High Priest also wore a crown made of pure gold.[6] On the crown was the inscription: HOLINESS TO THE LORD. The High Priest himself was required to be holy . . . he was representative before God of an entire nation that had been called to be "*a holy nation*"; a peculiar people, "a kingdom of priests."[7]

Again today, the Lord desires to see "Holiness to the Lord"

written over every area of our lives. We are to present our bodies as a living sacrifice, holy and acceptable unto Him (Romans 12). This includes all that we are: our intellect, the labors of our hands, the members of our bodies, the path of our feet, the intents of our heart, and the utterance of our lips. This purity of life can and must become our way of life, for we too are priests unto Him.

Time and time again Israel was warned, by their all-wise God, about the dangers of mixture and of co-mingling with the heathen all about. "For they have taken some of their daughters as wives for themselves and for their sons, so that the holy race has intermingled with the peoples of the lands; indeed the hands of the princes and the rulers have been foremost in this unfaithfulness."[8]

The same principles are essential in this day. There has been such tragedy from believers falling through influences from worldly friendships they refuse to break. Also, through becoming unequally yoked in marriage or business. The Lord doesn't mince His words when He expresses His heart on this pitfall and a flirtation with uncleanness.

"Therefore, come out from their midst and be separate," says the Lord. "And do not touch what is unclean ... And I will be a father to you, and you shall be sons and daughters to Me," says the Lord Almighty.[9]

Here again the Bible warns us about the dangers of mixture. Playing with fire through linking ourselves with unspiritual people: "Do not be bound (or yoked) together with unbelievers: for what partnership have righteousness and lawlessness, or what fellowship has light with darkness."[10]

In Jesus' messages to the seven churches, five out of the seven had *mixture.* He commends what is worthy of commendation, and then rebukes and warns. Accompanying these warnings is the urgent command to quickly repent. Unbelief, fear, false doctrine, compromise, and lukewarmness had crept in to contaminate the church. The Lord is warning, correcting, and judging, not in order to destroy, but for the purpose of lifting us to spiritual nobility. His people are to be a clear light in a dark world. One of the great problems delaying salvation for interested sinners is confusion from believers acting just like the worldlings.

The environment in which we live and work may make it hard for us to live with purity, but Jesus, our exemplary pattern, proved victory is fully attainable in the midst of immorality, ignorance, and hostility. God has provided the wherewithal to do likewise.

Draw near to God and He will draw near to you. Cleanse your hands . . . and purify your hearts. . . . [11]

When we do our part, He promises to give us power to overcome in an evil atmosphere. "I can do ALL THINGS through [Christ] who strengthens me."[12] Then again, "For whatever is born of God overcomes the world; and this is the victory that has overcome the world—our faith. And who is the one who overcomes the world, but he who believes that Jesus is the Son of God."[13]

The Word to the Ephesians (also to twentieth-century believers) is that the Lord will return only for a Church without spot or blemish. And "every man that hath this hope of seeing Him *purifieth himself."* [14]

The Beauty of Holiness—Unity

Since you have in obedience to the truth purified your souls for a sincere love of the brethren, fervently love one another from the heart.[15]

The beauty of holiness is also found in sharing one's life with other members of the Body. True love for the brethren is not exclusive—it is not independent. Jesus Himself, who never deviated from standards of holiness, intensely involved Himself in the lives of those around Him. He touched them, healed them, cheered them, taught them, and He forgave them. The

59

way of holiness through agape love is the way of selflessness. That includes being willing to humbly admit we don't know it all and that we haven't yet arrived, that we need the others in the Body. This is essential if we are to attain the full spectrum of Christ's brand of holiness in our life.

Holiness never involves being too busy for the widows or orphans. Too often in our day, we've relegated their care to the welfare agencies who seem more compassionate than some Christians. Charity is called "pure religion and undefiled"[16] when no personal gain is sought. The way we treat the needy and the lowly tells the world and tells God about our true spiritual character.

The Beauty of Holiness—Humility

Andrew Murray, discussing humility in daily life wrote,

> What a solemn thought, that our love to God will be measured by our every day intercourse with men and the love it displays; and that our love to God will be found to be a delusion, except as its truth is proved in standing the test of daily life with our fellow men. It is even so with our humility. It is easy to think we humble ourselves before God: humility toward men will be the only sufficient proof that our humility before God is real; that humility has taken up its abode in us, and become our very nature; that we actually, like Christ, have made ourselves of no reputation . . . the insignificances of daily life are the importances and the tests of eternity, because they prove what really is the Spirit that possesses us.[17]

God encourages us to be real people. To acknowledge that we are not gods but dependent creatures. That we did not make ourselves and have no basis for thinking the world should revolve around us. Self-centeredness must be elevated to a God-centeredness. Neither must we view our existence out of proper perspective, in some illusion of who we are. If we do, then our lives will be filled with torment and disappointments.

When we withdraw from the truth, a spiritual psychosis develops which utterly defeats the work God desires to perform in and through us. God cannot work with a spirit made haughty by an exaggerated estimation of self. That which is worthy in our lives is the Lord's praise alone.

> ...I say to every man among you not to think more highly of himself than he ought to think; but to think so as to have sound judgment...do not be haughty in mind, but associate with the lowly (of heart). Do not be wise in your own estimation.[18]

Pride is the very root of a person's desire to be unreal. And this unreal charade is often manifest in religious activities. Andrew Murray goes on to say, "Pride can clothe itself in the garments of praise or of penitence. ...in their spiritual history men may have had times of great humbling and brokenness, but what a different thing this is from being clothed with humility, from having an humble spirit, from having lowliness of heart...."[19]

Humility truly is a beauty of holiness. Humble men and women are like beautiful oases in today's vast desert of proud and selfish humans. A tormenting, inflamed ego never drives a mature believer. The peace and dynamic of Christ's humility marked His personality here on earth.

> Let the beauty of Jesus be seen in me
> All His wonderful passion and purity
> Oh Thou Spirit Divine
> All my nature refine
> 'Til the beauty of Jesus be seen in me.

If holiness consists in the emptying of ourselves so that God might live out His highest purposes through us, then humility is indispensable. If self-indulgence and unbridled selfishness were banished from this earth most insane asylums would stand empty.

> Do nothing from selfishness or empty conceit, but with humility of mind let each of you regard one another as more important than himself; do not merely look out

for your own personal interest, but also for the interests of others. Have this attitude in yourselves which was also in Christ Jesus, who, although He existed in the form of God, did not regard equality with God a thing to be grasped, but emptied Himself, taking the form of a bond-servant, and being made in the likeness of men. And being found in appearance as a man, He humbled Himself by becoming obedient to the point of death, even death on a cross.[20]

The ways of God when applied by any believer will ignite a beauty within for all men to see. The ultimate beauty formula! After Moses' encounter with God, his face was aglow for weeks afterwards.

In Ezekiel we read: "And thy renown went forth among the heathen for thy beauty: for it was perfect through my comeliness, which I had put upon thee, saith the Lord."[21] Zechariah saw that beauty in the Spirit. "They (His people) shall shine in His land as glittering jewels in a crown. How wonderful and beautiful all shall be!"[22]

Throughout the Bible there are numerous accounts of an awe by those who looked upon the shining countenance of angelic messengers. Invariably men and women in our day who have experienced the presence of the Lord or an angelic being likewise confirm this aura, great beauty and a great sense of holiness. Most of us have met a particularly godly person whose countenance glowed with a beauty of holiness.

Peter saw it in that awesome scene on the Mount of Transfiguration. The beauty Peter witnessed was, however, not just an outward effulgence, but it was translucent—emanating from the inner being of the "Second Adam"—the One who came to obey His Father. Moses and Elijah also were aglow with the beauty of holiness. In the triumphal scenes yet to come, John the Revelator paints the majestic portrait of Jesus as King of kings, describing "His face like the sun shining in its strength."[23]

Oh, worship the Lord in the beauty of His holiness. Stand in His presence with awe, all the earth.[24]

9

The Secret of Balance

For there is going to come a time when people won't listen to the truth, but will go around looking for teachers who will tell them just what they want to hear.[1]

No matter if it be the sweetest of notes, if that one note is played incessantly, isolated from the whole melody, it becomes noise. Likewise a truth when incessantly propagated to the exclusion of the full counsel of the Word, can become discordant. Remember that exhortation on the gifts of the Spirit being exercised apart from love? They become as sounding brass! Similar distortions can result from "Johnny-one-note" teaching.

Unhealthy Imbalance

Some months ago my wife, Virginia, and I were teaching at a series of meetings in Indiana. The teaching was on the theme: "Know ye not that the unrighteous shall not inherit the Kingdom of God?"

We stressed two verses from I Corinthians, "Know ye not that your bodies are the members of Christ? . . . " and "Know ye not that your body is the temple of the Holy Ghost?"[2] During the person-to-person ministry after one session, a young woman timidly approached me and said, "After hearing you tonight I am confused and embarrassed about it but I just have to share my problem with someone. I just couldn't leave the auditorium without seeking your counsel."

She poured out the problem she had been struggling with. She had been attending an enthusiastic home Bible study group during the previous year. During the recent months, her study group had been engrossed in extreme teaching in the area of submission. Overemphasis in one facet had produced an imbalance that had nearly swept her marriage away. Her dilemma had been compounded by a long series of messages at her church involving the *grace of God* and the New Testament saints' *liberty in Christ.* This series was based on the verse in Colossians which says, "Blotting out the handwriting of ordinances that was against us, which was contrary to us, and took it out of the way, nailing it to his cross."[3]

The failure of both the prayer group and her church to present *balanced* teaching on these themes ignited a tragedy in her marriage.

She went on to tell how her young Christian husband had foolishly begun to implement that liberty in Christ he was being taught. He began to revert to a life pattern he had indulged in before their marriage. Further, he began misapplying the prayer group's submission teaching, and insisted she join him every Friday night at a place where the entertainment featured an extremely lewd act roleplayed on a small stage. The wife became so troubled and conscience-stricken she confided in two of her closest women friends, who were also attending the "submission" studies. They were shocked by the situation, but reminded her of the principles of submission as being taught in their group. She was counseled to try to dissuade her husband, but if he still insisted, then it was her responsibility to submit to him. He was the head of their household and her covering. Further, they reasoned, it was the surest way to help him back out of this immoral pattern. If she were to have followed this line of submission, then she would also have been required to assist him in murder if he had required it of her!

I can still see her face. Few Christians I've met were more devastated than this troubled and torn young wife. Our counsel to her was to submit to her husband in all activities wherein they were permissible in the light of God's Word, but to make it clear to her husband that she could never again submit to such a grieving of God's Spirit which dwelt within her. It was evident that she had approached the edge of mental breakdown by trying to straddle the pit dug in her life by the convergence of two lines of unbalanced teaching.

Today's spiritual buffet is filled with many appealing teachings that, if overindulged in, will weaken certain Christians. Many, for example, are demonstrating an excessive appetite for the spiritual spectacular in meetings and even on Christian television. They have a weakness for easy solutions to life's complex problems. Being "slain in the Spirit," legitimate though it may be an occasion, can become just as ritualistic as other forms of worship.

There are no "finger snapping" formulas which can do away with life's real tests. Pressures and trouble are allowed by a wise Heavenly Father to hone and develop our characters. "Whom He loveth, He chasteneth." Jesus' disciples were never developed by "presto" Scripture-manipulating methods. Their spiritual stature grew while experiencing a thicket of problems, crises, and sufferings, just like you and me.

Trouble Is a Servant

All of us know trouble—at least I hope we do;
Trouble is a servant, but known as such to few.
We are taught to shun her and, if she comes too near,
Seldom do we face her but run away in fear.
Good and bad must meet her, the universe around—
Sinners, saints, kings and knaves—she comes where man is
    found.
Always make her serve you, for she can serve you well;

65

Just HOW you may use her your life will always tell.
Trouble is but passive—it's by our power to will
We make her either bless us or do the soul some ill.
How do you translate her from phrases filled with pain
To messages of strength—from loss to endless gain?
By faith we see behind the outer frightful mask
A servant in disguise, to do a gracious task.
Hearts may feel her wounding and life may suffer loss;
Faith translates her working, as freeing gold from dross.
Trouble will discover to any yielded heart
Hidden depths of power it only knew in part;
Sympathizing power, and love that understands;
Strength to help another with trouble-tested hands.
Trouble will release you from self and make you kind,
Adding new dimensions to heart and soul and mind.
Do not shun this servant, but look beyond her task
To beauty she will work—for which you daily ask.
Always see in trouble a chance to grow in grace,
Not a stroke of evil to hinder in your race.
Live the life triumphant above her fiery darts;
Rich fruitage will be yours to share with needy hearts.

—John Wright Follette

It might be profitable for those who are so sensitive about "negative confessions" to remember Paul taught, "For unto you it is given in the behalf of Christ, not only to believe on him, but also to *suffer* for his sake."[4] Paul didn't hesitate to confess that he "*pressed* toward the mark of the high calling"[5] on a road of life that was rutted with crises. He wasn't ashamed to report about these for fear some foolish Christian was gossiping that his problems were judgments of God because of some secret sin in his life.

Paul unashamedly wrote, "In stripes above measure, in prison more frequent, in deaths oft. Of the Jews five times received I forty stripes save one. Thrice was I beaten with rods,

66

once was I stoned, thrice I suffered shipwreck, a night and a day I have been in the deep; in journeyings often, in perils of waters, in perils of robbers, in perils by mine own countrymen, in perils by the heathen, in perils in the city, in perils in the wilderness, in perils in the sea, in perils among false brethren; in weariness and painfulness, in watchings often, in hunger and thirst, in fastings often, in cold and nakedness."[6]

No one dares attribute these to Paul's inability to walk in faith. The great Apostle's ministry sparkled with balance. In fact, balance is the most striking characteristic of Paul's writings. We see the sum of this in the fourth chapter of this same letter. "We are troubled on every side, yet not distressed; we are perplexed, but not in despair; persecuted, but not forsaken; cast down, but not destroyed . . . for our light affliction, which is but for a moment, worketh for us a far more exceeding and eternal weight of glory."[7]

Let's face it. Many have drifted into an appetite for the spectacular. There has been concern for this growing phenomenon over recent years. It became apparent at the big conferences where the crowds would surge to sessions which highlighted miracles, leg lengthening, being "slain in the Spirit" super faith, and prosperity teaching. The sessions offering teaching on discipline, growth-from-crisis, or holy living were sparsely attended.

Some holiness movements of the past overstressed externals: length of dress, the hair, no lipstick, no earrings, *ad nauseum*! Paul dismissed these human ordinances as being inadequate (Colossians 2). The better way is a transformation by the Spirit on the inside.

Jesus reacted to this spirit of majoring on the externals when He admonished those Pharisees who made spectacular public display of their fastings, prayer, and offerings. Jesus prayed, "Sanctify them through thy truth: thy word is truth."[8] He wants to see us purified at the heart level from within.

Paul wrote, "Be renewed in the spirit of your mind,"[9] or as

Derek Prince puts it, "Be brainwashed by the Holy Spirit ministering the Word to cleanse us inside out." Nevertheless, the Christian's appearance and behavior are evidence of conditions in the heart.

Two Congregations

The role of balanced teaching in the process of releasing or quenching the Spirit of God was dramatically illustrated during the past year in two different meetings where I spoke.

One of the moving hours of the year came during a conference in Shreveport, Louisiana. The Spirit had pressed me to depart from my announced theme, yet I was reluctant to speak on the new subject He was stressing me to preach. When I stood at the pulpit and finally discarded my notes, the Spirit of God filled the sanctuary. My knees began to shake. God had shown me how the revival could reach undreamed of new heights if we would reembrace the beauty of holiness. I feared the congregation would be disappointed and reject the holiness teaching at a conference billed, "Thanksgiving."

Stalling for a few minutes with greetings, I haltingly began to speak on the "dreaded theme" of Christian righteousness here in this sophisticated age. Then it happened . . .

The next 55 minutes were like thunder and lightning. I felt detached from the message which was coming from my own lips. Its thrust came like surgery from a loving scalpel in the hand of God. The Spirit warned about superficiality in ministry today, God exposed willingness of many to adjust to the sin all about us, and some believers' unabashed flirtations with sin itself.

The congregation remained dead quiet. I feared they were stunned with disappointment of such a stern theme. Then, I heard scuffling and soft moaning coming from the choir seats just behind. I continued. Then, from several different locations in the main audience, came the same scuffling and the moaning. Suddenly I knew we were experiencing something I had only read about. This "something" had happened back in the Whitfield, Finney, and Billy Sunday meetings: people slipping to the floor and weeping under a conviction. I finished and returned to my seat. But before I ever made it, the Lord began to speak in prophecy through Nolan Logan, the pastor. The words underscored and extended the Lord's passionate call for a renewal of holiness among His people. At the close of that prophetic message, the entire congregation leaped to their feet with the most incredible and persistent clapping! They were applauding the beauty of His holiness.

God convinced me in that hour that His people are hungry for "strong meat." That they are to march flying banners of purity, holiness, and the fear of God.

Dozens in that wonderful congregation shook my hand and said, "Thank you, thank you, Mr. Otis, for bringing that message; Christians have been waiting so long to hear that again." My heart was singing!

In contrast to the response of the Shreveport congregation to God's new call to holiness was that of a different audience in the Northwest a few weeks later. This scene occurred during an annual world convention of a church denomination at the Portland, Oregon Civic Auditorium.

Among the several thousand present at the Sunday evening session to which I spoke were hundreds of pastors and missionaries. Again I felt a stirring by the Lord to share the call to holiness. During the opening minutes of my message, I carefully pointed out that God was not diminishing His provisions of grace and that a new emphasis on holiness was under no circumstances to be interpreted as an effort to "bring back the Law." But since God's moral law proceeds from the never-changing righteousness of God, holiness cannot be cast out from our teachings. The Spirit eloquently pleaded in that session for Christians to love grace, long-suffering, forgiveness, and liberty, but to balance all this with exhortation against the malignant sin which has crept into the Body of Christ. When I

69

returned to my seat, silence again filled the auditorium. I was convinced God was breaking through again to this congregation filled with ministers.

But too often those directing a service are afraid of silence in a meeting. The Lord wanted us to meditate on His call to righteousness during that precious hush, and to just quietly savor the beauty of His Holiness. The leader, however, was unnerved by both the message and the stillness over the congregation. He leaped to the microphone and shouted, "Stand on your feet! Now, for Jesus, let's give seven big cheers for 'grace!'"

Obediently the congregation stood and gave seven shouts of "grace." But such timid shouts. The leader cried, "Stand again. Now for Jesus, let's give one great shout for 'liberty.'" They did.

God's thrust for that session was all but erased in a minute. Oh, that we may learn to love His holiness with the same zeal as we have for Jesus' grace, liberty, and forgiveness.

The Splitting of Time

But some may say, "Whoa there, George! You are trying to bring back the Law. Don't you remember those ordinances were nailed to the cross? We are in a new dispensation, under a new covenant. You're writing like we never got out of the Old Testament. This is the twentieth century! That Law business doesn't apply anymore."

Like a high wire artist, the spiritual walk requires continual balance. Somewhere along the line we slipped off on such a grace and liberty emphasis that we forgot Jesus said He did not come to do away with the Law but to fulfill it.

This is the covenant that I will make with them after those days, saith the Lord; I will put my laws into their hearts, and in their minds will I write them.[10]

Our Heavenly Father never threw out the Old Testament, nor did He intend grace to become a fuel for the flames of sin.

70

Some Christians have developed a near-paranoia about "bringing back the Law." But grace, liberty, and forgiveness are never threatened by holy thought, righteous living, or the preaching of purity. Grace and righteousness were never intended by Christ to be an either/or proposition—"For, dear brothers, you have been given freedom: not freedom to do wrong, but freedom to love and serve each other."[11]

Today, when we discuss holiness with some Christians there is a bristling—a fear that legalism or bondage will be laid on them. But following Jesus' life, and following His teachings on *holiness*, never brings bondage—but life—more abundantly. The power of this revival will never reach the potential God intended until the component of holiness is given its rightful proportion.

When we consider typical Christian attitudes concerning the Old Testament teaching on holiness, we detect a serious deception: that sometime a couple thousand years ago God changed His mind about righteous living and that this "mindshift" by God split time between B.C. and A.D. As though the righteous God of the Old Testament was replaced by His "more tolerant" Son. It is almost as though they believed God's emphasis lurched in the New Testament away from holiness to liberty. But righteousness and liberty aren't either/or matters. God expects righteousness and provides grace.

In God, there is no variableness—no shadow of turning. He is the same yesterday, today, and forever. Jesus came to personally live before us the righteous ways of His Father. He also became an adequate and final sacrifice for our sin. He perfectly did both. To simplify, the New Testament era brought change in the old covenant ceremonial sacrifices. They are no longer in need since Jesus was the ultimate sacrifice. But it never connoted a diminishing of the moral law or of God's view of sin and righteousness. In other words, the letter of the Law is superseded by the Spirit of the Law which God implanted within us through Christ.

The New Testament emphasis on holiness and righteousness is, if anything, even stronger. The New Testament contains more on righteousness than all the verses on the gifts of the Spirit, miracles, baptisms, communion, and salvation—all put together! The New Testament itself is our "holiness manual."

Let's reread a few excerpts from the New Testament:

Know ye not the unrighteous shall not inherit the kingdom of God?...

For the wrath of God is revealed from heaven against all ungodliness and unrighteousness of man...

If any man defile the temple of God (your body) him shall God destroy....No whoremonger, nor unclean person...hath any inheritance in the kingdom of Christ...but the face of the Lord is against them that do evil...for because of these things cometh the wrath of God upon the children of disobedience...

For if we sin wilfully after that we have received the knowledge of the truth, there remaineth no more sacrifice for sins... [12]

The New Testament is loud and clear that the God of the New Testament and the God of the Old Testament are one and the same...and that sin is just as abhorrent to Him in our day as it was in the days of Sodom.

10
About Judging

Behold, how good and how pleasant it is for brothers to
dwell together in unity![1]

Especially while ministering overseas, one of the questions
I am most frequently asked concerns the fragmentation of
Christianity. Typically, unbelievers will cite hundreds of organizations and denominations all professing to be "brothers in
Christ." A Buddhist once said to me, "You Christians spend
more energy fighting each other than the devil. You have erected a thousand walls to keep yourselves apart. If Christians
would ever pull together, they would take the world."

I didn't have the heart to tell him, "Not only do we have our
different denominations and sects fragmenting unity, but even
individual members within the Body dissipate enormous energy in criticism and gossip about one another." Oh, how Satan
labors to keep God's people weakened through divisions!
Judgmental criticism is so counterproductive toward advancing
Christ's Kingdom. The ego gets some kind of charge by judging
another person's imperfections. How much better if we would
search our *own* hearts and audit our own deeds. Paul wrote,
"Let a man examine himself. . . . If we would judge ourselves,
we should not be judged."[2]

When Jesus interceded for the adulterous woman at her stoning, His line of inquiry toward her accusers focused on their own qualifications to be her judge. "He who is without sin among you, let him be the first to throw a stone at her."[3] Of course, her accusers all slipped away. Matthew wrote, "Judge not, that ye be not judged. For with what judgment ye judge, ye shall be judged. . . . "[4]

I have often been caught up short by the Spirit when He would show me I was judging other Christians for failures that were common to myself. This is a widespread problem among believers. God's harshest judgments are upon those who judge others for sins they too are guilty of. The Bible says, "And thinkest thou this, O man, that judgest them which doeth such things, and doest the same, that thou shalt escape the judgment of God?"[5]

Do you remember where, in II Samuel, God used Nathan to trap King David in just such an episode?

The scene took place shortly after David had facilitated Uriah's death in order to secure his wife, Bathsheba, for himself. Nathan, the prophet, then went before David and recited the case of a rich and powerful man stealing a certain poor man's only lamb. Nathan asked the king to render judgment concerning this case. David, with his hands still dirty from the unrepented sin with Uriah's wife, pompously delivered judgment against the lamb-stealer, "As the Lord liveth, the man that hath done this thing shall surely die." Nathan, looking steadfastly into the eyes of the guilty king said, "Thou art the man!"[6]

The hour is late. Most Bible scholars would agree we are now approaching the edge of time. Soon the trump of God shall blast and its sound heard throughout the earth. Christ is pleading through His personal messenger, the Holy Spirit, for His Bride to prepare herself for the wedding supper, urging us to ready our garments till they are without spot or wrinkle. And the Groom is calling for a Bride aglow with the beauty of holiness, a Bride who has cared enough about that meeting with her Beloved to look critically at herself and correct those spiritual imperfections and soil while there is still time.

And now, little children, abide in Him, so that if He should appear, we may have confidence and not shrink away from Him in shame at His coming.[7]

The Bridegroom certainly doesn't want a Bride torn by suspicion, criticism, hatred, and division. No Groom cares to marry an immature Bride whose ways and thoughts are ever critical and suspicious. And God the Father isn't going to contaminate a holy Heaven with either the deceiver or the unholy.

We need to understand just how seriously God views everything which threatens the cohesiveness between members of His household. After all, each member is being shaped as a vital component in God's ultimate dwelling place.

You also, as living stones, are being built up as a spiritual house. . . . [8]

In whom the whole building, being fitted together is growing into a holy temple in the Lord; in whom you also are being built together into a dwelling of God.[9]

The cement which holds together these "living stones" of God's dwelling is *love*. That cement of unity becomes very strong when we prefer one another, believe the best, and live out the fruit of the Spirit toward other believers.

Creating this eternal cement for God's dwelling place was behind Paul's teaching to the Ephesians, "I . . . entreat you to walk in a manner worthy of the calling with which you have been called, with all humility and gentleness, with patience showing forbearance to one another in love, being diligent to preserve the unity. . . . "[10]

The Apostle labored to preserve unity in the early church that they might thereby stand victoriously in the face of hostility. "Now I beseech you, brethren, by the name of our Lord Jesus Christ, that ye all speak the same thing, and that there be no divisions among you. . . . "[11] Paul never hesitated to speak out against people who were threatening love and unity. "Mark them which cause division ... and avoid them!"[12]

Where Christians Are to Judge

What has been covered thus far doesn't mean we are not to pass judgment upon any human conduct. We have just reviewed some of the areas where Scripture warns we are *not* to judge. But God has given the ability to discern between right and wrong that we might be equipped to judge wherein is the believer's prerogative. The Scriptures quickened by the Spirit will sensitize the believer to right and wrong. With surefire guidance from God's written Word we can know what is contrary to the law of Christ. Mature Christians are those "who by reason of use have their senses exercised to discern between good and evil."[13]

This is a compendium of subjects of which believers are instructed to judge.

Do Judge—Our Own Hearts: Paul wrote, "So let a man examine himself." We're encouraged to take a look at ourselves —an analytical look. Not psychoanalysis, but a Spirit-directed audit into our own hearts and motives. We are to judge or "examine" our behavior in light of these motives. (Proverbs 4:23—"Watch over your heart with all diligence ... ") Now this isn't always as easy as it sounds. "The heart is deceitful ... and desperately wicked: who can know it?"[14] Fortunately, all is not lost—it is most assuredly not a hopeless case—the Bible provides the solution. Ask God to look for us. "God ... knoweth the hearts ... God trieth the hearts and reins ... Search me, O God, and know my heart: try me ... and see if there be any wicked way in me."[15]

We must be willing to stay quiet long enough to give the Spirit adequate time to answer. If more within the Body of Christ would ask for a Divine picture of their heart rather than external blessings, this nation would undergo a spiritual revolution.

Do Judge—The Exercise of the Gifts: Because of the great power and influence of various gifts of the Spirit, God has provided guidelines on how they should be manifested. Prophecy, for example, as mentioned in I Corinthians 14:29: "Let the prophets speak two or three, and *let the other judge.*" We are to discern whether or not a message is indeed from God. God does not want His people to be gullible and presumptuous. It is important here to note that it is the *message*—not the *person*—that is judged. God does not want us to turn into critical skeptics, but He also doesn't want us to act on the basis of a "word" given in the flesh.

> Thus saith the Lord of hosts, Hearken not unto the words of the prophets that prophesy unto you; they make you vain: they speak a vision of their own heart, and not out of the mouth of the Lord.[16]

Do Judge—Candidates for Church Appointment: Paul in his letter to Timothy lays out in detail the necessary qualifications of one who would seek church office. After finishing his list he exhorts: "And let these also first be proved (judged/tried) then let them use the office of a deacon, being found blameless." There is obvious wisdom in exercising sound judgment in this type of situation. History reveals the heartache of many a church too hasty and eager in elevating the wrong individual to an office of responsibility. Many churches and missions are still today staffed by incompetent and ungodly leaders who do not measure up to scriptural standards, all because they failed to judge at the time of selection. Frankly, to *not* judge in this case is not only unwise ... it is sinful.

In his book, *Of God and Men,* A. W. Tozer says, "We languish for men who feel themselves expendable in the warfare of the soul, who cannot be frightened by threats because they have already died to the allurements of this world ... they will not be forced to do things by the squeeze of circumstances; their only compulsion will come from within—and above.

"This kind of freedom is necessary if we are to have prophets in our pulpit again instead of mascots. These free men will serve God and mankind from motives too high to be understood by the rank and file of religious retainers who today shuttle in and out of the sanctuary. They will make no decisions out of fear, take no course out of a desire to please, accept no service (solely) for financial considerations . . . nor will they allow themselves to be influenced by a love of publicity or the desire for reputation . . . the church at this moment needs men, the right kind of men, bold men."[17]

Do Judge—Doctrine: Again wisdom dictates that we are not to believe everything we hear. There are all manner of people preaching all manner of things these days. We are subjected today to such a volume of teaching from seminars, tapes, sermons, TV, and books. Most are sound but they are primarily man's interpretation of God's Word. Modern Christians must avoid becoming religious "vacuum cleaners" without discerning truth from error. Carefully *judge* all in relation to the Scriptures. Those desiring spiritual integrity could well follow the wise Berean Christians, "examining the Scriptures daily, to see whether these things were so."[18] Lazy Christians, who consistently feed off the result of others' Bible research, run a risk of themselves being deluded. "All Scripture is inspired by God and profitable for . . . training in righteousness."[19]

The Bible puts stress on the discerning of doctrine. Paul urged Timothy to "remain on at Ephesus, in order that (he) may instruct certain men not to teach strange doctrines."[20] It is sobering to consider the potential for deception in our day. Paul warned about this and feared just such a time when believers would fall for error and exotic practices. "The time will come when they (Christians) will not endure sound doctrine; but wanting to have their ears tickled, they will accumulate for themselves teachers in accordance to their own desires; and will turn away their ears from the truth, and will turn aside to myths."[21]

Another vital thing we can do to keep from falling prey to wrong doctrines (other than daily devouring God's Word) is to live the truths we have already learned. After "having our senses trained to discern good and evil."

Do Judge—False and Deceptive Ministries: The Lord warned us that the world would in the latter days be full of false prophets. It is another area in which the Word of God admonishes us to exercise judgment. "Beloved, believe not every spirit, but *try the spirits* (judge) whether they are of God: because many false prophets are gone out into the world."[22]

People are so fearful today about judging in this realm that false ministries have grown like wild weeds in our midst. The longer we wait to recognize them and *pull them out,* the further they can spread. The atmosphere within parts of the Body of Christ has become almost carnival. Various teachers, evangelists, and miracle workers hawk unsound personal gospels. A tolerant attitude toward false ministries allows them to snare the unlearned. Believers upon detecting serious error are to be like the watchman on the wall. Go first to the errant minister, if unresponsive to the elders, then to the whole body.

In the book of Revelation, God commends the church at Ephesus for their strong stand against false apostles. "I know your deeds and your toil and perseverance, and that you cannot endure evil men, and *you put to the test* those who call themselves apostles, and they are not, and you found them to be false."[23]

The best way to discern deception is to stay close to Jesus and His infallible book. When a false prophet comes near, you will sense the grief in your heart. Watch for *love, humility* and *integrity* in the different ministries. Where these qualities are *genuinely* present ("by their fruits ye shall know them") it is a strong indicator that the ministry bears the stamp of God.

Do Judge—Legal Disagreements Between Brethren: "Does any one of you, when he has a case against his neighbor, dare

79

to go to law before the unrighteous, and not before the saints? Or do you not know that the saints will judge the world? And if the world is judged by you, are you not competent to constitute the smallest law courts? Do you not know that we shall judge angels? How much more, matters of this life? I say this to your shame. Is it so, that there is not among you one wise man who will be *able to decide* between his brethren . . . ?"[24]

Paul here is asking a series of rhetorical questions to emphasize his point. God requires Christians to settle their differences within the household of God. Why would they be judged by the unrighteous (civil courts) when the brethren were full of the Holy Spirit and had access to all Heaven's wisdom? It's still a good question. And should be repeated: "Why in the world don't we recognize the tremendous advantage we already have (in the Body) for problem-solving?"

We see little practice of Paul's wishes today. We do see individual Christians, churches, and even missions, fighting and accusing one another in the courts, dragging down the name of our Lord Jesus with them. The land is overrun with lawyers and the court dockets overcrowded. So let every believer avoid the public realm and speedily settle disputes within the privacy of God's family. Let us each help to judge between disputing brethren.

Do Judge — Sin in the Body: In the fifth chapter of I Corinthians is an incident which Paul uses to teach on the subject of church discipline. One of the Corinthian church members was involved in an incestuous relationship with his father's wife. The church, instead of "judging" or administering discipline, was rather proud of their liberality toward the sinner. Paul, in his exhortation, declares that even though he is absent in body, he has "already *judged* him who has so committed this, as though (he) were present."

Paul wrote, "For what have I to do with judging outsiders? Do you not judge those who are within the church?" God has revealed His methods for church discipline. The problem today is that too many of God's people and their shepherds have neither the inclination nor the disposition to deal in matters of holy living and discipline.

Gross sin is allowed to enter our sanctuaries under the notion that "love covers all." Failing to recall that God's Word plainly declares, "He that covereth his sin shall not prosper,"[25] the Bible commands, "Reject a factious man after a first and second warning, knowing that such a man is perverted and is sinning. . . ."[26]

So long as sin is left unconfronted, we are proving that we love so little we would rather see the soul damned than interfere. Paul raised yet another question to those content to let sin fester unmolested within the Body: "Do you not know that a little leaven leavens the *whole lump* of dough?"[27]

Sin is not benign . . . it is malignant! God's Word teaches that sin must be confronted. If after confronting the individual there is no repentance, there is to be a severance of the "leaven" from the Body. "Clean out the old leaven, that you may be a new lump. . . ."[28] This is done for two reasons: first, to protect the whole Body from being infected by malignant, destructive sin; and secondly, to provoke deep thought on the part of the unrepentant sinner. Through such discipline, repentance may bring eventual restoration. In abstaining from our duties to judge sin within the Body, we actually violate the words of Christ and His Body.

Don't *Judge—Another Believer's Heart:* What the Scriptures fervently warn against is judging the *motive* or heart intention of fellow believers. Only God can see into the heart. Since we have but limited knowledge of facts and circumstances, we are warned to withhold our judgment of another's motives. "Therefore do not go on passing judgment before the time, but wait until the Lord comes who will both bring to light the things hidden in the darkness and disclose the motives of men's hearts; and then each man's praise will come to him from God."[29]

When we are not sure, always give other Christians the benefit of the doubt.

> Could we but draw back the curtains that surround
>   each other's lives,
> See the naked heart and spirit, know what spur the
>   action gives . . .
> Often we should find it better, purer, than we think we
>   should:
> We should love each other better if we only understood.

And so, wanting to please our Lord who so loved us that He gave His only begotten Son: Let us love one another out of a PURE HEART fervently.[30]

11
The Little Foxes

Bang the drum slowly... revival is dying... the thunder of His power is rolling away, distantly sounding "Be ye holy as I am holy...."

It's usually not too difficult for Christians to recognize and avoid the big and obvious sins. What separates the "spiritual giants" from the rest of us—the men from the boys, you might say—is integrity, their integrity in the daily, lesser choices.

Repetitive "little" sins sap the believers' spiritual vitality, paving the way toward greater disobedience. This is why the Bible warns us to head them off at the thought stage, cutting them off by "casting down imaginations and every high thing that exalteth itself against the knowledge of God, and bringing into captivity every thought to the obedience of Christ."[1]

Fuzzbusting

Not long ago I was speaking in a large Florida city. The weather was muggy and just as the meeting ended, a spectacular electrical display made a beautiful climax.

My host had assigned a young man to drive my wife and me to our motel for the night. We hopped into a large van he used to service Christian bookstores over a sprawling 300 mile radius. Soon we were rocketing down the highway talking about his work while he drove.

Suddenly I interrupted him. "Say, we've been chattering so intently you've slipped above the speed limit. We're doing over 70—did you realize it?"

His response was unexpected. "Mr. Otis, we don't have to worry about the speed at all. Let me demonstrate." He then reached under the dashboard with his right hand and flipped a switch. Within a few minutes, a light on the panel of a little box began to flash with authority! My new friend pointed to the light with obvious glee as his foot eased up sharply on the accelerator. In seconds we had slowed to 50 MPH.

He explained, "It's called a 'Fuzzbuster.' That light indicator just warned there is a police car up ahead with radar speed detections."

Sure enough, in less than a mile, we cruised past a "black and white" parked along the edge of the highway.

He laughingly crowed, "I bought it so I could handle more territory for the Lord!"

My response to him came slowly. My mind was tumbling with thoughts about the subtlety of our adversary and the spiritual gullibility of some believers.

Finally I said, "Burt, would you pray about using that radar detector? When you stop to analyze what you are doing with it, I'm afraid you'll discover that you are rationalizing away lawlessness."

In the book of Romans, we are told that those who are charged with enforcing the law receive their authority from God Himself. In fact, one translation concludes with ... "and they do not wear the sword in vain." Too many Christians fudge on all kinds of traffic regulations and we must recognize this as sin. Furthermore, when we cheat on a traffic law, it remains sin whether we are caught or not! To break any law in the guise of helping God is an offense to His moral sensibilities.

84

More Than a Glance

The other day I saw a full-figured girl wearing a T-shirt with the inscription: "Looking is free but touching will cost you." We have all, at one time or another, heard some foolish woman, upon seeing her husband eyeing an attractive woman, say, "It's okay to look, honey, but no handling of the merchandise!"

But you and I know better. Sin begins in the mind. Sexual fantasizing is dangerous regardless of liberal psychologists' approval. Jesus declared that it is an adulterous sin to look upon a woman with lustful imaginations.[2]

King David's most crushing failure began when he "oggled" another man's wife whose body was carelessly uncovered. Her name was Bathsheba. The passions which arose in David's heart upon looking at Bathsheba burned until he had caused her husband to be murdered. The Bible says, "Can a man take fire in his bosom and not be burned?"[3]

Mugging Ma Bell

Many in God's family seem vulnerable to rationalizing transgressions involving their employer, government agencies or big business. There is a subconscious temptation to consider such as "fair game" and to take little advantages.

Some years ago I discovered a little plan being used to save money in my own office. My secretary was driving to Virginia on her vacation. The girl filling in for her wanted daily telephone contact in order to ask about matters which only my secretary would know about. But they didn't want me to have to pay long distance charges if no emergency had arisen. So, by prearrangement, my secretary would call in collect once a day, and, if no emergency existed, her collect call was refused—to avoid phone charges. Only if my secretary was needed to answer some question was her collect call accepted.

This is one of those subtle things. You might ask, "What was wrong with that?" Well, upon careful examination they were using Ma Bell's long distance operators and her billion dollar phone network without charge on the days my secretary's calls were refused. The girls were earnestly trying to save our ministry some money and never once thought of their scheme as cheating the phone company.

In a similar case a minister friend made it a regular habit to ignore the operator on person-to-person phone calls, while aggressively extracting information out of other parties . . . without charge, of course. It won't stand God's test, will it?

Have you ever played "free telephone games" and never before thought of it as stealing?

Evangelistically Speaking

Little foxes are sometimes even found in the pulpit. On occasion guest evangelists and teachers are "short changed." While most churches exercise great integrity, a great number of traveling ministers have experienced a problem along this line. The pastor will arise and make an impassioned plea for a generous offering especially for the guest speaker. When the evangelist leaves the church, an offering check for $25 may be handed to him. The pastor has skimmed money from the offering to use for other church needs.

This may sound minor, but it is a serious breach of integrity which can impoverish the church more than the guest speaker. Ananias and Sapphira paid with their lives for "lying to the Holy Ghost" about a money matter. It is a serious matter for a ministry to use monies given for a specific project for other uses.

"Righteous" Rip-Offs

Another danger area for moral carelessness often lies in the realm of our jobs. The Bible instructs believers to show loyalty, integrity and industriousness toward their employers. The Bible says: "Whatsoever thy hand findeth to do, do it with all thy might, as unto the Lord."[4] God is grieved when one of His own children sloughs off and does just enough to get by at his job.

Too often Christians will witness, swap testimonies, or even read Christian books while being paid by their company to work. It is a subtle deception causing them to feel very spiritual for doing it.

When we do things other than our assigned job during working hours without permission, it is a form of robbery and God cannot approve. Performing secular tasks efficiently and "as unto the Lord" is true spirituality.

Likewise, rationalizing the use of "sick pay" to skip work in order to go to a Christian meeting doesn't square with God's ways. "The Company" often seems so impersonal that we are tempted to take what we can get away with.

Those little foxes creep in so many ways: late starting work, carrying things home, bad-mouthing the company, padding the expense account, using company phones or stamps for personal use, and so on.

Being a worthy servant to our employer is honoring to the Name of Christ. Our place of work represents one of the best arenas in life to set a standard of excellence so that He may be exalted.

Those Who Live by the Sword . . .

I don't remember hearing any minister cover the delicate subject we are about to write upon, but it must be discussed. When the Apostle Paul interfered with the guilds of idol-makers in Ephesus the city broke out with riots. This is a touchy subject. Few involved in labor unionism have ever even thought of its activities as being questionable. During this century segments of the labor movement commendably healed an area of human injustice. A goodly portion of its work has been noble and many workers have greatly benefited.

However, Christians who are members of certain of today's labor unions must continually seek divine guidance about their ongoing involvement. This originally noble cause has, in some instances, taken on ominous characteristics. The pendulum has swung from benevolence to malevolence in many unions. Coercion, theft, violence, sabotage, corruption and even murder (for example, Jimmy Hoffa) have recently become the means by which they operate. The prince of this world is the one who comes to rob, to kill, and to destroy. Christians concede that certain unions have taken on characteristics of the evil one, but alibi that they aren't personally involved with these venomous tactics. But how will the Righteous Judge view a believer if he accepts extorted fruits and fails to influence his own union leadership? The thought is worthy of meditation.

Unemployment Benefits

All too often we encounter believers finagling on unemployment pay. The government seems so impersonal, doesn't it? Earlier this year I received a phone call from a Christian woman who had been doing some sparetime typing at her home for several different firms. She said, "Mr. Otis, my husband and I have decided to take a few months off to visit relatives in the Midwest. I am going to apply for unemployment checks to help us financially while we are away on our visit. When the unemployment people mail you the forms, please mark them to indicate I was laid off."

Somehow there's an extra temptation to feed the little foxes when it comes to matters involving Uncle Sam. Another 33-year-old Christian friend quit her job last year because it was interfering with two home Bible study and prayer groups she was attending. She then applied for unemployment benefits and lived for six months off the checks. Never once did it seem to occur to her that she was living a deception. This woman was willing to let other taxpayers finance her "spiritual" pursuits, though she was able-bodied. As you would suspect she wore a super-spiritual air for this "sacrifice" for Jesus.

Wholesome Diversions

How often the Bible cites the great benefits from spending time before God and in His Word. Yet in our pleasure-oriented society, opportunities to neglect the spiritual seem omnipresent. Television, bowling, hobbies, bridge, fishing, golf, flying, novels, telephone-gabbing ... to name just a few!

There are many leisure activities which contain no inherent immorality. Yet when anything begins to seriously intrude on our spiritual time it should become suspect. Could there be some "wholesome diversion" in your own life which has crept in to become a kind of god?

Whenever we find anything overly dominating our thoughts and personal schedule, it should be reexamined. Many who have lost their first love for God will find that "innocent" little foxes have been spoiling their vines. "Seek ye first the Kingdom of God and His righteousness and all these things shall be added unto you."[5]

Benefit of Hindsight

It is embarrassing to admit how long I was personally a member of that chorus of believers who scoffed at "those old holiness people." We joked about their overemphasis on the externals: dress, jewelry, movies, alcohol, hair styles, dancing. "How misguided," we said, "such killjoys, don't they know about our liberty in Christ?"

We had a point.

So did they! With the benefit of hindsight it is apparent many of those holiness preachers were visionaries. In the spirit, they had seen the latent perils to our generation arising from moral compromises. Their concerns have since proven valid.

Many of the grace and liberty scoffers are now struggling with the fruit of situation ethics: bikini believers, wine bibbers and TV garbage swillers. Many Christians are not the least hesitant to watch movies containing segments of moral decadence.

That which is taken in through the eyes and ears affects the health of the soul exactly like junk food taken in through the mouth affects our physical body. If we can sit through program after program on secular TV, and freely attend modern-day motion pictures, it is probable the moral discernment has become dulled.

Little foxes are lurking everywhere: manipulations on tax forms; padding insurance claims; broken promises; cheating on exams; gossip, and so forth.

God speaks so often in His Word about honest weights and measures. He continually monitors the integrity of believers. He longs for a people who will think and act with purity like Himself.

It would be profitable to audit our own lives—searching for "little foxes" which may have crept in. The exciting realization is this: conquer the "little" sins and the big ones can never again so easily overwhelm us.

Some have suffered with persistent problems for many months and are puzzled at God's failure to answer their prayers. It may be, upon closer examination, that these little foxes are holding up the answer. The Bible says if we regard (permit) iniquity in our heart God will not even hear our prayers.[6]

A little season of fox hunting may break loose a new clap of victory thunder in our lives.

Tallyho!

etc . . .

12
Human Rights

"Our commitment to human rights must be absolute..." [1] "We ought to be a beacon light on human rights to the rest of the world..." [2] so spoke the newly sworn-in President, Jimmy Carter. The subsequent story is now well known. The human rights issue quickly became the hallmark of the Carter Administration's foreign policy although the issue, even in its contemporary setting, didn't originate with Jimmy Carter.

In August of 1975, 32 European nations along with Canada, the United States, and the Soviet Union gathered in Helsinki's Finlandia House to sign what are often referred to as the Helsinki Accords. The so-called "Basket Three" agreement stated in part: 'The participating states will respect human rights and fundamental freedoms..." President Carter simply gave public notice to the issue.

Everyone, it seems (with the exception of totalitarian bureaucrats), is finding that "rights" rhetoric fits like a glove. How could anyone even vaguely interested in a reputation not take a stance supportive of individual rights? This is particularly true of our democractically enlightened generation who fancy themselves viewing history's abuses from their lofty twentieth-century perch. Demonstrating a flair for moral sophistication, our twentieth-century crusaders are unleashing a torrent of oaths, vowing to correct the abuses of history during their lifetime. In righting one wrong they vicariously free all slaves that ever were.

The "I Deserve" Syndrome

If we are going to fight for human rights it is necessary that we begin by determining the extent of those rights. Negligence at this point will result in our defending a quagmire of mixed motives that contains a hefty portion of wants and greeds along with legitimate rights.

Thanks to President Carter's outspokenness on behalf of human rights (many of them unquestionably legitimate), thousands of individuals and special interest groups have found the public ear to be more sensitive to their various causes so long as their goals are pursued as "rights."

The civic urge toward unrestrained indulgence is frightening. The once-trim structure of a disciplined people flourishing under the practice of self-limitation is now grotesquely swollen, intoxicated by the serpent's poison purchased from her medicine men. Robert J. Ringer, best selling author and the common man's Ayn Rand, is one of them; peddling his glorified selfishness with no regrets. His smash best seller (one year on the N.Y. Times best seller list) Looking Out For #1 was "dedicated to the hope that somewhere in our universe there exists a civilization whose inhabitants possess sole dominion over their own lives . . ." Ringer confidently goes on to tell us, "You will always act selfishly, no matter how vehemently you resist or protest to the contrary, because such action is automatic. You have no choice in the matter." [3] With a public sympathetic to the cry for rights and the "inevitability" of selfish behavior, we are presented with the necessary ingredients for the "I deserve" syndrome.

We are living in a day in which it is far easier to discuss rights than responsibilities. This day however has been steadily approaching us for some time. "During the past fourteen years," for example, "the number of citizens living on welfare has *increased 500%*." [4] Senator Jesse Helms citing the spendthrift habits of liberal bureaucrats stated, "Washington (is) interested in setting up a leisure class, subsidized by the labors of their countrymen." [5]

Capitalizing on yesterday's abuses, today's rights crusaders have become shrewd masters in the art of exploiting exploitation. What often began as an effort to obtain equality or justice winds up in the long run as a lust for *dominance*. In the pursuit of one's "rights" the focus has a tendency to become self-centered. Here again the "I deserve" syndrome enters the picture. The "right" to a "fair shake" is rarely the objective. Because so many hours have been spent contemplating past abuses and lost benefits, a mere *correction* of the situation doesn't satisfy—it's not enough. Once we begin to pursue our "rights," focusing on what is "due" us, a spirit of selfishness takes control. A vindictive desire for retroactive ransom fills the heart.

This has been the great temptation of racial minorities. For years now our ears have been filled with the demands of various black and Chicano organizations. We've been told how the road to freedom and equality has been blocked by racist (oh how this word defies definition!) empire preservers. The high proportion of black and brown prison inmates, it is so unequivocally pointed out, is conclusive evidence of political slavery and violated human rights.

It is unnerving when you consider the extent to which the rights movement has affected sound judgment. We are now hearing recurring statements of support for the "rights" of criminal prisoners. Inmates in recent days have rampaged throughout prisons rioting, burning and killing in order to call attention to their "deprivation." These temper tantrums are duly noted by various "rights" organizations and liberal politicians who subsequently make concerted efforts to appease these individuals whose rights and dignity have been so trampled upon. In one recent case officials at the Vacaville Correctional Facility (California), demonstrating great humanitarian concern, supplied 13 transsexual inmates with female hormones and brassieres. Phil Guthrie, a spokesman for the State Department of Corrections, said that the transsexual prisoners are not allowed to wear skirts, however. Dr. Gene Prout, the facility's chief medical officer, added he knew the program was controversial, but said: "It is established as the ethically and morally proper thing to do..." [6]

Isn't it interesting how criminal prisoners are inclined to be selective when they talk about rights? They often seem to omit any mention of the rights of their victims. Not much is said about the fact that in many cases their victims can no longer plead for their rights because they no longer exist.

Gay libbers have also mounted the media platform. Their rantings and ravings and bold protestations have made homosexuality news. The pattern of logic posed by Gay liberationists is uniform all across the nation. "It has been carefully designed and scripted to accomplish their objectives: to win sympathy, tolerance and even public support for homosexuality while shaming and shouting their critics into silence." [7] Here's a verbatim example:

> "I don't want you to like me. I just want you to get out of my way. I'm an American citizen. I want my human and civil rights ... you are our problem. You are our problem. I have no problems. You're the problem ... I'll tell you what. If you change the laws tomorrow in this land ... and you make it as equal for Gay people as it is for anyone else in this land, I'll quit and you'll never hear from me again. But as long as there's oppression, buddy, you're gonna' hear from me and I'm gonna' keep on fightin' ... I'm fightin' awfully hard ... whatever the cause (of homosexuality) is, is irrelevant when you're talking about human rights ... it's none of your

96

business what my body's made for...just leave me alone! Christian prejudice astounds me...your hypocrisy is amazing...you have no need to be afraid of me, to condemn me, except your Bible says homosexuality is a sin...that's just another myth...one of many myths in the Bible. Thinking people are too smart for that anymore...that kind of thinking went out with kerosene lamps...your mind is too small and brittle for enlightened people...all we want is our human rights." [8]

Homosexuals have unleashed a very public effort to blackball their arch-enemy Anita Bryant. One of the techniques has been a boycott of Florida Orange Juice for which Mrs. Bryant has made a number of commercials. A homosexual spokesman announced the boycott would continue, " 'Either until the industry terminates her employment or she stops doing what she's doing...' In other words, the very people who posture that Gayness is not a case of moral right or wrong, but one of civil rights, are willing to actively work to deny someone else's civil rights." [9]

More and more women are joining the ranks of "the sisterhood," adding their voices to the collective cry for liberation. "Sisterhood in a pre-revolutionary society is women attempting to collectivize our responsibilities so as to overcome our isolation and give us the time and energy necessary to struggle together to build the revolution." [10] The collective cry was heard in a new way recently as some 400 women picked different musical notes and held them. The eerie monotones reverberated against the walls of the theatre of Performing Arts at the University of California's Santa Cruz campus. This was a call to "The Goddess." Later in the day, encouraged by bongo drums, spontaneous groups of circling women danced bare-breasted. What they started is called the *Goddess Movement* or *Womenspirit!* Christine Downing, head of San Diego State University's Religious Studies Department, estimates that many—if not most—"spiritually sensitive" women in their movement are willing to replace the biblical God with a frankly pagan and polytheistic approach.

The demands of the feminist movement are staggering, in quantity as well as quality. The heavily Marxist oriented resolutions of the liberationists reveal an insatiable appetite for independence and ultimately—domination.

• Male society has sold us the idea of marriage . . . we must work to destroy it. The end of the institution of marriage is a necessary condition for the liberation of women. Therefore it is important for us to encourage women to leave their husbands . . .[11]

• NOW (National Organization of Women) demands the removal of such derogatory terms as bastard, illegitimate, and unwed mother from national, state and local statutes . . .

• (In divorce cases) where support is not immediately forthcoming from the assessed spouse, that courts order such payments be paid immediately from public funds . . .

• (Children) should not be channeled into a role based on sexual stereotypes. Further research must be undertaken to discover ways to prevent sex-role channeling.

• Resolved that upon dissolution of a marriage, the dependent spouse should be guaranteed health and accident insurance by the government (and) government-sponsored retraining for re-entry into the job market.

• NOW opposes any state, federal, county or municipal employment law or program giving special preference to veterans.

• Resolved that the wife should be able to keep her own name or the husband to take the wife's name, and/or there should be the option of both partners choosing a neutral second name to be used also by the children.

• A woman's title should be "Ms" without differentiation as to marriage, and a woman should use her given first name.

• Because the wearing of a headcovering by women at religious services is a symbol of subjection within many churches, NOW recommends that all chapters undertake an effort to have all women participate in a "national unveiling" by sending their headcoverings to the task force chairman. At the spring meeting of the task force of women and religion, these veils will be publicly burned.

• No other woman suffers more abuse and discrimination for the right to be her own person than does the Lesbian . . . because she is so oppressed and so exploited, the Lesbian has been referred to as "the rage of all women condensed to the point of explosion." This rage found a natural outlet in the women's liberation movement . . . therefore, be it resolved that a woman's right to her own person includes the right to define and express her own sexuality and to choose her own lifestyle and be it further resolved that NOW acknowledge the oppression of Lesbians as a legitimate concern of feminism.[12]

Ratification of the Equal Rights Amendment will not end the feminist clamor—just as passage of the Civil Rights Act did little to appease American blacks. As long as you're "getting"— why stop? The rationale behind the milking of society is the "I deserve" syndrome. To terminate a crusade simply because a major goal is realized would not only put the crusaders out of a job but it would leave them in a vacuum. The dynamic in these various rights crusades lies not in the demands themselves but in the *process of demanding.* It is power, not peace that is coveted.

Out in the blistering hot San Joaquin Valley, Enos Pryor walks dejectedly under the symmetrical rows of his lush fruit trees. The price of food has been escalating at dizzying pace, and millions around the world hover near death from starvation. Yet Enos' vast orchards hang heavy. There is such a bumper crop that dozens of fruit-laden limbs have broken.

But Enos Pryor's day of harvest has come and gone. Now the fruit is worthless. He is about to lose the farm he has nurtured for 40 years. Why? Because not a single picker has cast a shadow in his orchard for the harvest. Pickets have seen to that.

The thick night clouds hanging over the city turn red from eight separate fires. Not one fire siren can be heard. Not one fire truck responds to the reported fires. After one of those fires, Elbert and Charlotta Sprague huddle beside their two small children, staring in glassy-eyed trauma at the collapsing skeleton of their home.

Why had all the fire engines set mockingly in their fire stations while eight fires burned unchecked across the city?

The firemen wanted a raise.

Union strikes have managed to disrupt nearly every level of modern life; education, transportation, food, production, sports and protection have all been hit. Air traffic controllers have repeatedly made life miserable for travelers (especially in Europe) ruining countless long-anticipated and hard-earned vacations through their slowdowns and strikes. For many years our nation has witnessed strikes staged by mine workers, steel workers, farm and auto workers all of whom negotiate "in good faith" and are always "willing to avert a walkout." In recent times, however, a very disturbing trend has developed that threatens to usher the United States into anarchy. Various union workers employed in roles vital to the everyday well-being of society are now taking it upon themselves to force the public to "cry uncle." This type of extortion however is old stuff to England—the workers' paradise. Britain, as any internationally-minded American knows, has been virtually paralyzed by the unions. Not too long ago British firefighters staged a nationwide walkout resulting in enormous losses. Perhaps this was encouragement to the United States brotherhood. Police and firefighters have walked off their jobs in New York, Cleveland and Memphis in recent days, leaving their communities helpless in the face of uncontrolled fire, looting and assault.

Those public servants entrusted with the responsibility of enforcing the law have themselves become lawless, ignoring curfews and court injunctions.

All of this is then promulgated in the guise of human rights. This type of union action we are told is brought on (100 percent of the time) by self-serving obstinate management. We hear it's really a matter of fairness—nothing more, nothing less: "We're only after what we deserve." (Recent union pension fund scandals would seem to indicate that, perhaps, not everyone is willing to exercise such restraint!)

The key to fending off all moral limitations is to discover ways to remain convinced that your pursuits are legitimate. If this can be accomplished you will then be able to plug your ears to all "moral static." The leaders of the feminist movement recognize and encourage this. "Because our lives are committed to the service of our sisters and to building a people's revolution we are not afraid of criticism. No matter who gives it . . ." [13] Robert Ringer adds some further suggestions. "Clear your mind, then forget foundationless traditions, forget the 'moral' standards others may have tried to cram down your throat, forget the beliefs people may have tried to intimidate you into accepting as 'right.' Allow your intellect to take control . . . and, most important, think of yourself—Number One." [14]

Humanism—Foundation of the Rights Movement

Solzhenitsyn, in his magnificent Harvard speech, traced the decline of Western civilization back to its roots which he diagnosed as "rationalistic humanism or humanistic autonomy." He further defined humanistic autonomy as "the proclaimed and enforced autonomy of man from any higher force above him."

Autonomy. If one word could sum up the essence of the current struggle for rights, this one comes mighty close. When viewed alongside some of its dictionary synonyms (independent, self-contained, self-ruling) our conviction grows even bolder. And how at home this word seems in the humanist manifesto!

"We affirm that moral values derive their source from human experience. Ethics is autonomous and situation-

101

al, needing no theological or ideological sanction." [15]

Harry Conn in his book, *Four Trojan Horses*,[16] provides us with an interesting glimpse into the "humanist factories" of America. "Another humanist principle is the belief in the right of maximum autonomy...the right to do one's own thing, whatever it may be...some time ago in the county in which I live, there was an uproar over a questionnaire administered in the schools by Johns Hopkins University. Parents were outraged by the many questions that invaded student and family privacy. Parents were justified in their outrage, but they completely overlooked the purpose behind the questionnaire, which was to determine how autonomous the students were becoming! A report issued by Johns Hopkins explained that one of the goals of 'open education,' which is a euphemism for humanistic education, was to develop self-reliance and autonomous behavior. The report stated, 'A major part of the growing up process is developing a willingness to act autonomously ...'"

How rapidly a developed willingness can become a flaming passion. Many of the various rights movements today openly and proudly admit their endeavors are based on humanistic principles. Mr. Conn goes on to quote a University of Chicago professor, "If you want to take away people's freedom of choice, you start yourself a HUMAN RIGHTS MOVEMENT. Certainly, people will eventually catch on to your hypocrisy, but by that time it is usually too late for them to stop you." [17]

Humanism Is Not Humanitarian

So often these two words are used interchangeably. Yet no two words could have more divergent meanings.* A humanitar-

---

*This follows the general definition of the word *humanitarian*—"concerned with human welfare"—not the philosophical derivative of humanism-humanitarianism, which states that "man may perfect his own nature without divine aid."

ian is concerned with his fellow man; a humanist is concerned with himself—Number One. Man divorced from a Higher Being becomes a law unto himself. There is no one above him to set the rules or establish the guidelines—he himself is sovereign. The inherent danger of the humanist philosophy is described in Solzhenitsyn's *Gulag Archipelago*. "Power is a poison well known for thousands of years. If only no one were ever to acquire material power over others! But to the human being who has faith in some force that holds dominion over all of us, and who is therefore conscious of his own limitations, power is not necessarily fatal. For those, however, who are unaware of any higher sphere, (humanist's for example) it is a deadly poison. For them there is no antidote." [18]

A humanist has no motivation to be humanitarian. There is no appeal to selflessness, no virtuous inclinations. The upshot of *humanist thinking,* as Malcolm Muggeridge duly points out, is a dearth of *humanitarian performance.* "I've spent a number of years in India and Africa, where I found much righteous endeavor undertaken by Christians of all denominations; but I never, as it happens, came across a hospital or orphanage run by the Fabian Society or a Humanist leper colony." [19]

A False Assumption

When self-gratification is embraced as a personal end in life, certain problems are bound to arise. Unfortunately for pleasure seekers emotions do not operate without intellectual stimuli. In other words, emotions respond to what the mind thinks upon. The pursuit of sensual gratification has in this way harnessed many a mind—and emotions can be a hard taskmaster. "Anyone who suggest(s) that the pursuit of happiness (that disastrous phrase written almost by chance into the American Declaration of Independence, and usually signifying in practice the pursuit of pleasure as expressed in the contemporary cult of eroticism) runs directly contrary to the Christian way of life as conveyed in the New Testament, is sure to be con-

103

demned as a life-hater ... "[20] Actually, quite the contrary is true. Those individuals who practice restraint in life are often those who live life to the brim ... who love life to the fullest.

Our problem is that we equate experience with happiness. We mistakenly believe that the individual who experiences the most in life is the one who understands true freedom. Liberation! We need to realize liberty alone without the exercise of wholesome restraint becomes license. License, in turn, all too often leads to bondage which evaporates freedom. Solzhenitsyn speaking from personal experience, relates that often physical detention provided the greatest environment for moral-spiritual freedom. On the whole, it is conversely true that the quest of many Americans (and a varied assortment of other human beings) after the rudiments of pleasure, proclaimed as liberty and protected as human rights, has led to moral and spiritual bondage.

"Almost all popular books and plays assume that personal happiness is the legitimate end of the dramatic human struggle. The doctrine of man's inalienable right to happiness is anti-God and its wide acceptance by society tells us something about that same society. In the New Testament the emphasis is not upon happiness but upon holiness. God is more concerned with the state of people's hearts than with the state of their feelings. Undoubtedly the will of God brings final happiness to those who obey, but the most important matter is not how happy we are but how holy."[21]

Holiness As Emptiness

Do nothing from selfishness or empty conceit, but with humility of mind let each of you regard one another as more important than himself; do not merely look out for your own personal interests, but also for the interests of others. Have this attitude in yourselves which was also in Christ Jesus, who, although He existed in the form of God, did not regard *equality* with God a thing to be grasped, but emptied* Himself, taking the form of

---

*or laid aside His privileges.

104

a bond-servant, and being made in the likeness of men. And being found in appearance as a man, He humbled Himself by becoming obedient to the point of death ... "[22]

So you want to be Christlike? Well, Paul has certainly given us a graphic description of "this attitude." It's as though Paul got to thinking, after he had admonished the Philippians to "do nothing from selfishness," that they needed a positive, practical *example* to undergird the admonition. So he said, "Have this attitude in *you* which was also in Christ Jesus." Let's examine this attitude in light of the modern day clamor for rights.

Verse 6 reveals a significant piece of evidence about Christ's attitude toward the "I deserve" syndrome. It states, "Although He existed in the form of God (He) did not regard EQUALITY with God a thing to be GRASPED." He did not attempt to hang on to what was rightfully His. Not only did He not grasp equality but He "emptied Himself," laying aside all privileges and giving up all personal rights. As if this wasn't enough He took on the form of a servant and further humbled Himself—even to the point of death, which Andrew Murray points out is the highest proof of humility's perfection. And, Murray goes on to say, "this life of entire self-abnegation, of absolute submission and dependence upon the Father's will, Christ found to be one of perfect peace and joy. He lost nothing by giving all to God. God honored His trust, and did all for Him, and then exalted Him."[23]

How different this Christ-attitude is from the world-attitude. All around us people are grasping, clawing and screaming for equality. The individual "I demand" has given way to the belligerently growing "we demand" of collective selfishness. The mere mention of relinquishing what is "rightfully" ours pushes defense mechanisms into high gear. We live in a "get what you deserve" age. And once again enter Mr. Robert Ringer, the Number One purveyor of quotable selfishness. His you-won't-get-credit-for-it theory states, "Don't do something for the reason that it's 'the right thing to do' if there's no benefit to be derived from it."[24]

"One of Jesus' greatest gifts was to release a tidal wave of humility flowing through the world against the devil's contrary tide of self-assertion."[25] Jesus who became of no reputation out of love for us desires to work that same attitude out in our hearts. There is a rest—a peace found in self-denial. It takes enormous energy to maintain the selfish boundaries of one's "territory" and "rightful" possessions. The selfless man, on the other hand, is free from forever defending himself, because he, like Christ, has no reputation, he has no fear of losing it, and he can go about his Father's business.

How wonderful it is to be around Jesus. The wise and tender Master who says, "Learn from Me; for I am gentle and humble in heart; and you shall find rest for your souls."[26]

So many require, as Mother Basilea Schlink so appropriately puts it, that we "burn incense to their egos." After a full day in a world of swollen, demanding egos, how sweet it is to rest in the presence of the humble and gentle heart of Jesus.

"If once we learn that to be nothing before God is the glory of the creature, the spirit of Jesus, the joy of Heaven, we shall welcome with our whole heart the discipline we may have in serving even those who try or vex us. When our own heart is set upon this . . . we shall study each word of Jesus on self-abasement with new zest, and no place will be too low, and no stooping too deep, and no service too mean or too long continued, if we may but share and prove the fellowship with Him who spake, 'I am among you as He that serveth.' Brethren, here is the path to the higher life. Down, lower down!"[27]

13
The Club of Rome

Men from various nations of the world board flights headed for a mutual destination. These, however, are no ordinary men. They are the eminent scientists, historians, philosophers and leaders in the world, known loosely as The Club of Rome. They meet informally and somewhat arbitrarily to discuss major world problems. After rounds of discussion and debate, a statement is issued expressing the sense of this distinguished body of scholars.

Wouldn't it be exciting if we could assemble eminent Christian thinkers of our day, set them around a table, and interview them? We're going to do just that! We "invited" three distinguished Christian minds to our hypothetical interview.

Malcom Muggeridge's life has revolved around two major establishments—education and journalism. Schooled at Cambridge, Mr. Muggeridge later taught for a season at the Egyptian University in Cairo. Then in 1967-1968 he served as Director of Edinburgh University. Malcolm Muggeridge's journalistic trek included stops at the *Manchester Guardian* (which included a stint as a Moscow correspondent), the *Daily Telegraph* and as editor of the fount of satire—*Punch* magazine. Using BBC cameras or editorial columns for his pulpit, Malcolm Muggeridge has become known as one of the world's thorniest social critics. The conversion of this eloquent socialist to Christ, needless to say, rocked England to its heels. Following his conversion he authored several books, notably, *Jesus Rediscovered, Jesus the Man Who Lives,* and *Christ and the Media.*

Alexander Solzhenitsyn, has, of course, gained worldwide attention as Russia's reluctant exile, the "king of the dissidents." Alexander Solzhenitsyn lived through scenes that few men survive to tell about. In his best selling book, *The Gulag Archipelago,* he reveals the staggering brutality and inhumanity of a previously obscure segment of history. What makes Solzhenitsyn different from other historians, however, lies in his interpretation of the facts and events that have changed the course of so many lives. It was, during those interminable years in prison, that he acquired the keen spiritual insight that has become so familiar to us today.

> But passing here between being and nothingness,
> stumbling and clutching at the edge,
> I look behind me with a grateful tremor
> upon the life that I have lived.
>
> Not with good judgment nor with desire
> are its twists and turns illumined.
> But with the glow of the higher meaning
> which became apparent to me only later.
>
> And now with measuring cup returned to me,
> scooping up the living water,
> God of the universe! I believe again!
> Though I renounced you, you were with me!

Dr. Francis Schaeffer is without a doubt one of the foremost evangelical thinkers of today. As a philosopher and theologian, Dr. Schaeffer has affected countless lives. Fortunately for the world he is a prolific writer. Books like *The God Who Is There, He is There and He is Not Silent* and *How Shall We Then Live?* have answered questions men have raised for centuries. Along with his wife Edith, Dr. Schaeffer founded the

L'Abri Christian Communities where scores of young travelers with restless minds have found rest.

In the following interview we have carefully tailored our questions to enable each one of our "guests" to speak for themselves. Their answers represent the thrust of each individual. Let's take advantage of this unique opportunity to compare the thoughts of these great Christian spokesmen.

INTERVIEWER

"Gentlemen, I wonder if we could begin by asking each of you to comment on the present composition and direction of Western society. What trends, if any, do you see? Are there signs, as we have heard, that this generation is in trouble?"

MUGGERIDGE

"Caesar Augustus, at the height of his fame had already been proclaimed a god, with appropriate rites for worshipping him; and his regime was considered to be so enlightened, stable and prosperous that it would go on forever. A final solution to the problems of government and a guarantee of the continuing happiness and prosperity of all who were fortunate enough to be Roman citizens. Expiring civilizations are prone to such fantasies, for instance, ours. . . . "[1]

SOLZHENITSYN

"Clearly, whatever feelings predominate in the members of a given society at a given moment in time, they will serve to color the whole of that society and determine its moral character. And if there is nothing good there to pervade that society, it will destroy itself, or be brutalized by the triumph of evil instincts . . . "[2]

INTERVIEWER

"How did the West decline from its triumphal march to its

present sickness? The mistake must be at the root, at the very basis of human thinking in the past centuries. An erroneous world view became the basis for government and social science, and could be defined as rationalistic humanism or humanistic autonomy: The proclaimed and enforced autonomy of man from any higher force above him. It based modern Western civilization on the dangerous need to worship man and his material needs. However, in early democracies, as in American democracy at the time of its birth, all individual human rights were granted because man is God's creature. That is, freedom was given to the individual conditionally, in the assumption of his constant religious responsibility. Subsequently, however, all such limitations were discarded ... a total liberation occurred from the moral heritage of Christian centuries ... the West ended up by truly enforcing human rights, sometimes even excessively, but man's sense of responsibility to God and society grew dimmer and dimmer."[3]

SCHAEFFER

"As the memory of the Christian base grows dimmer, freedom will disintegrate ... the system will not simply go on, divorced from its founding roots. And the drift will tend to be the same, no matter what political party is voted in. When the principles are gone, there remains only expediency at any price. ... The attempt to be autonomous—to be independent from God and from what He has taught in the Bible and from the revelation of God in Christ—affects the political leaders as well as the university professors and the common people. ... Absolute principles have little or no meaning in the place to which the decline of Western thought has come."[4]

INTERVIEWER

"Mr. Solzhenitsyn, Dr. Schaeffer mentioned a moment ago his concern over the potential disintegration of human freedom. You alluded to this same theme with a remark I found most intriguing and I'd like to ask you to elaborate if you would. You talked about the fact the West has ended up enforcing human rights excessively. How then would *you* define freedom?"

SOLZHENITSYN

"Genuine human freedom is inner freedom, given to us by God: freedom to decide upon our own acts, as well as moral responsibility for them.[5]

"Here is the true Christian definition of freedom. Freedom is self-restriction! Restriction of the self for the sake of others! Once understood and adopted, this principle diverts us—as individuals, in all forms of human association, societies and nations—from outward to inward development, thereby giving us greater spiritual depth. The turn toward inward development, the triumph of inwardness over outwardness, if it ever happens, will be a great turning point in the history of mankind . . . if in some places this is destined to be a revolutionary process, these revolutions will not be like earlier ones—physical, bloody and never beneficial—but will be moral revolutions, requiring both courage and sacrifice . . . "[6]

INTERVIEWER

"Mr. Muggeridge, what significance do you place in this moral revolution?"

MUGGERIDGE

"The Christian religion and (its) values no longer prevail; they no longer mean anything at all to ordinary people. Some suppose that you can have a Christian civilization without Christian values. I disbelieve this. I think that the basis of order is a moral order; if there is no moral order there will be no political or social order, and we see this happening. This is how civilizations end . . . pockets of revived interest in the church scarce-

111

ly offset the otherwise prevailing apathy."[7]

MUGGERIDGE

"Public benevolence can never be a substitute for private virtue.... I recognize that the motive is often admirable; unfortunately the result is almost invariably the exact opposite of what's intended. Posterity (assuming there is one) is likely, in my opinion, to see liberalism and all its legislative and social consequences as the working out of a collective death-wish. They will not otherwise be able to account for the fact that, in its name, the essential Christian foundations of European civilization were systematically undermined, its strength dissipated, and the moral, social and political order it had evolved irretrievably shattered."[8]

INTERVIEWER

"Dr. Schaeffer, what about this prevailing apathy that Malcolm speaks of? Is it true? If so, what, if anything, can we do about it?"

SCHAEFFER

"We must not forget that the world is on fire. We are not only losing The Church, but our entire culture as well. We live in a post-Christian world which is under the judgment of God. I believe today that we must speak as Jeremiah."[9]

INTERVIEWER

"What are the alternatives to not speaking out?"

SOLZHENITSYN

"In keeping silent about evil, in burying it so deep within us that no sign of it appears on the surface, we are implanting it, and it will rise up a thousandfold in the future."[10]

SCHAEFFER

"We are not excused from speaking, just because the culture and society no longer rest as much as they once did on Christian thinking. Moreover, Christians do not need to be in the majority in order to influence society."[11]

INTERVIEWER

"Dr. Schaeffer, what in your opinion does the Church need to do in order to regain its influence?"

SCHAEFFER

" ... The Church must be known simultaneously for its purity of doctrine and the reality of its community ... exhibition of the love of God in practice is beautiful and must be there. The heart of these principles is to show forth the love of God and the holiness of God simultaneously ... if we stress the love of God without the holiness of God it turns out only to be compromise. But if we stress the holiness of God without the love of God, we practice something that is hard and lacks beauty."[12]

SOLZHENITSYN

"It is open to everyone of us, whether learned or not, to choose—and profitably choose—not to evade the examination of social phenomena with reference to the categories of individual spiritual life and individual ethics."[13]

How may we interpret this impromptu interview with the eminent voices of Christianity? Certainly we hear the strains of Jeremiah. Yet not without hope! We have been warned in three-part harmony. Yet not without direction! The civilization which we call ours is unmistakably showing signs of wear. The moral refurbishing required to once again exhibit respectability will no doubt be costly. That choice, however, is still within our power. If we can begin by acknowledging that the solution is volitional and not chronological, we may perchance witness a resurrection in our day.

Lord, grant us the resolve to make those hard choices, or at least give us insight into the alternatives.

Footnotes

Chapter 1
1. Jeremiah 6:14, 15
2. Jeremiah 5:31
3. Proverbs 14:34a
4. Luke 21:25 (NASB)
5. See II Kings 22—23.
6. Ezekiel 2:7 (NASB)

Chapter 2
1. Matthew 23:24, 27
2. Ezekiel 9:1-3
3. Ezekiel 9:3b-6

Chapter 3
1. See Colossians 1:17.
2. Psalm 8:3
3. Psalm 24:3
4. Psalm 24:4
5. See Hebrews 11.
6. James 1:17
7. Acts 15:12
8. See John 14:12.
9. Matthew 5:6

Chapter 4
1. II Timothy 4:4
2. Esther 4:14
3. Isaiah 6:5
4. See Revelation 3:16.
5. I Kings 18:21 (NASB)
6. Matthew 6:21
7. Luke 12:16-20

Chapter 6
1. Revelation 3:14-17
2. Joshua 24:15
3. Acts 17:6
4. Luke 22:42b (NASB)
5. James 1:8
6. See Exodus 20:3.

Chapter 7

1. See II Chronicles 16:9.
2. I Peter 3:12 (NASB)
3. Deuteronomy 6:24 (NASB)
4. Isaiah 40:28
5. Isaiah 40:12 (NASB)
6. See Song of Solomon 2:10, 11; 4:6.
7. Isaiah 61:10, 11
8. See Psalm 103:7
9. Exodus 33:11 (See also Numbers 12:8.)
10. James 1:17
11. Psalm 5:4
12. Ezekiel 18:32
13. Psalm 5:5
14. Psalm 94:16
15. Jonah 4:2 (NASB)

Chapter 8

1. I Chronicles 16:29
2. Ecclesiastes 7:29 (NASB)
3. Romans 8:29
4. II Corinthians 3:18
5. Matthew 5:8
6. See Exodus 28:36, 38; 39:30, 31.
7. Exodus 19:5, 6
8. Ezra 9:2 (See also Leviticus 18:30 and Deuteronomy 7:6.)
9. II Corinthians 6:17 (NASB)
10. II Corinthians 6:14 (NASB)
11. James 4:8 (NASB)
12. Philippians 4:13 (NASB)
13. I John 5:4, 5 (NASB)
14. I John 3:3
15. I Peter 1:22 (NASB)
16. James 1:27
17. Andrew Murray, *The Humility of Holiness* (Spire), p. 34.
18. Romans 12:3, 16
19. Murray, *The Humility of Holiness*, p. 41, 42.
20. Philippians 2:3-8 (NASB)
21. Ezekiel 16:14
22. Zechariah 9:16, 17 (NASB)
23. Revelation 1:16 (NASB)
24. See Psalm 96:9.

Chapter 9

1. II Timothy 4:3 (TLB)
2. I Corinthians 6:15, 19
3. Colossians 2:14
4. Philippians 1:29
5. See Philippians 3:14.
6. II Corinthians 11:23-27
7. II Corinthians 4:8, 9, 17
8. John 17:17
9. Ephesians 4:23
10. Hebrews 10:16
11. Galatians 5:13 (TLB)
12. I Corinthians 6:9; Romans 1:18; I Corinthians 3:17; Ephesians 5:5; I Peter 3:12; Ephesians 5:6; Hebrews 10:26

Chapter 10

1. Psalm 133:1 (NASB)
2. I Corinthians 11:28, 31
3. John 8:6 (NASB)
4. Matthew 7:1, 2
5. Romans 2:3
6. II Samuel 12:5, 7
7. I John 2:28 (NASB)
8. I Peter 2:5
9. Ephesians 2:21, 22 (NASB)
10. Ephesians 4:1-3 (NASB)
11. I Corinthians 1:10
12. Romans 16:17
13. Hebrews 5:14
14. Jeremiah 17:9
15. Acts 15:8; Psalm 139:23, 24; Psalm 7:9
16. Jeremiah 23:16
17. A. W. Tozer, *Of God and Men* (Christian Publications), pp. 14, 15.
18. Acts 17:11b (NASB)
19. II Timothy 3:16 (NASB)
20. I Timothy 1:3
21. II Timothy 4:3, 4 (NASB)
22. I John 4:1
23. Revelation 2:2
24. I Corinthians 6:1-3, 5 (NASB)
25. Proverbs 28:13a

26. See Titus 3:10.
27. I Corinthians 5:6 (NASB)
28. I Corinthians 5:7a (NASB)
29. I Corinthians 4:5 (NASB)
30. See I Peter 1:22.

Chapter 11

1. II Corinthians 10:5
2. Matthew 5:28
3. Proverbs 6:27 (NASB)
4. Ecclesiastes 9:10
5. Matthew 6:33
6. Psalm 66:18

Chapter 12

1. Quoted in *Los Angeles Herald-Examiner* Editorial, Aug. 12, 1977.
2. *Los Angeles Herald-Examiner*, April 22, 1977.
3. Robert J. Ringer, *Looking Out for #1* (Fawcett Crest), p. 46.
4. U.S. Senator Jesse Helms, *When Free Men Shall Stand* (Zondervan), p. 73.
5. Ibid., p. 74.
6. Associated Press report, *Los Angeles Times.*
7. William D. Rodgers, *The Gay Invasion* (Accent) p. 55.
8. Ibid., pp. 51-54.
9. Ibid., p. 57.
10. *The Document: A Declaration of Feminism*—(N.O.W.), p. 23.
11. Ibid., p. 11.
12. *Revolution: Tomorrow Is NOW*—(N.O.W.), pp. 5-6, 15-17, 20-21.
13. *The Document: A Declaration of Feminism*, p. 22.
14. Ringer, *Looking Out for #1, p. 8.*
15. *The Humanist Manifesto* (Prometheus Books), p. 17.
16. Published by Bible Voice, Inc. (Excerpt quoted from p. 82, "The Religion of Humanism in Public Schools" by Barbara Morris.)
17. Harry Conn, *Four Trojan Horses* (Bible Voice), p. 148.
18. Alexander Solzhenitsyn, *The Gulag Archipelago.*
19. Malcolm Muggeridge, *Jesus Rediscovered* (Tyndale House), p. 157.
20. Ibid., p. 114.
21. A. W. Tozer, *Of God and Men* (Christian Publications), p. 45.
22. Philippians 2:3-8 (NASB)
23. Andrew Murray, *Humility—The Beauty of Holiness* (Spire), p. 21.
24. Ringer, *Looking Out for #1*, p. 88.
25. Malcolm Muggeridge, *Jesus the Man Who Lives* (Fontana), p. 153.

26. Matthew 11:29 (NASB)

27. Murray, *Humility—The Beauty of Holiness*, p. 27.

Chapter 13

1. Malcolm Muggeridge, *Jesus the Man Who Lives* (Fontana), pp. 31, 32.
2. Alexander Solzhenitsyn, *From Under the Rubble* (Bantam), p. 104.
3. *Time* magazine, July 19, 1978.
4. Francis Schaeffer, *How Shall We Then Live?* (Revell), pp. 250, 251.
5. *U.S. News & World Report*, Oct. 13, 1976.
6. Solzhenitsyn, *From Under the Rubble*, p. 136.
7. Malcolm Muggeridge, *Jesus Rediscovered* (Tyndale House), pp. 235, 164.
8. Ibid., p. 158.
9. Francis Schaeffer, *The Church Before the Watching World* (Inter-Varsity), p. 69.
10. Alexander Solzhenitsyn, *The Gulag Archipelago* (Harper and Row), p. 178.
11. Schaeffer, *How Shall We Then Live?*, p. 256.
12. Schaeffer, *The Church Before the Watching World*, p. 54.
13. Solzhenitsyn, *From Under the Rubble*, p. 105.

Other books by George Otis:

- —THE BLUE PRINT
- —CRISIS AMERICA
- —ELDRIDGE CLEAVER: ICE & FIRE
- —GHOST OF HAGAR
- —GOD MONEY AND YOU
- —GOD THE HOLY SPIRIT
- —HIGH ADVENTURE
- —JESUS 220 NAMES
- —MILLENNIUM MAN
- —PEACE, POWER AND HAPPINESS
- —TERROR AT TENERIFE
- —YOU SHALL RECEIVE
- —RHODESIA: THE SMOKE THAT THUNDERS

If you wish to write Mr. Otis
address your letter to:

George Otis
P.O. Box 7491
Van Nuys, Ca 91409

The publisher would like to express gratitude to Muriel Delaplane for permission to use her portrait of the author on the back cover of this book. "Cookie" Delaplane is ranked among the top ten living portrait artists. She is a gifted woman, equally at ease in the White House and on the ancient streets of Jerusalem. Miss Delaplane's portrait of the great artist Olaf Wieghorst has been acclaimed as one of the truly sensitive and fine works of art. "Cookie" Delaplane developed her own unique portrait style playing a cool pigment against warm pigments; a technique which makes colors vibrate from the canvas. The backgrounds, though subtle, are alive with color, seemingly three dimensional. Although her portraits are not "tight," they are executed with a freedom of style based on extreme honesty and strength of lines. For truly distinguished portrait work, Muriel Delaplane may be reached at her studio home in Stuart, Florida.